ECKHART PUBLIC LIBRARY
AUBURN, INDIANA
925-2414

HERITAGE OF DEDICATION

Heritage

of

Dedication

Agnes Dubbs Hays

One Hundred Years
of the
National Woman's Christian Temperance Union
1874-1974

SIGNAL PRESS

Evanston, Illinois

1973

Mrs. Annie Turner Wittenmyer
First President
1874-1879

FOREWORD

We are now ready to release and send on its way this little volume entitled "HERITAGE OF DEDICATION." We bespeak for it a hearty welcome from the public, but more especially from the members of the National Woman's Christian Temperance Union.

In thinking over those who might be able to produce such a publication, the National Officers unaminously suggested the name of Mrs. Glenn G. Hays, former National President and now President Emeritus of the organization. We felt she would have the time, the clarity of thought, the ability to make research and the talented pen to inscribe her feelings; thus to make a historical, readable, interesting book for the present and future generations. Each chapter is self contained, thus to be included in the monthly program planner, though the book as a whole, may be read and reviewed to present a historic, factual, enlightening program for special centennial emphasis.

No one, unaccustomed to writing, can imagine the immense amount of labor and patient, painstaking research required to glean the facts contained between these covers. Within these pages are well authenticated statements of actual work accomplished in the face of difficulties, and apathy of public opinion, which would have daunted less heroic or determined women than enlisted in this peaceful warfare, "for God and Home and Everyland." The author has not relied upon her memory in writing this history. All statements recorded are substantiated, as you will see by the notes appended to this book. In her research she was substantially aided by the bound copies of the minutes of the annual meetings of the organization, the annual addresses of the presidents, the recorded resolutions and recommendations. Also copies of THE UNION SIGNAL (official publication) were diligently searched for items of historic interest that they might be made available and preserved in the 100 year history. News clippings in file, other temperance journals recording items of interest, and copies of the Congressional Record, found their place among the copy to be researched. All of these have been the most efficient and effective help in securing material for the record.

For many years Mrs. Hays has been one of the foremost leaders in the Woman's Christian Temperance Union, having been honored with leadership in local, state and national WCTU organizations. She is also actively affiliated with PEN WOMEN, a national organization of women writers. She emerges from a strong temperance family background. Possessed of a master mind, keen intellect, forceful logic, she is recognized as a leader in much good and useful work. She is far-sighted and practical in her plans, such plans having brought a worthwhile measure of success to her co-workers in the departments of the WCTU. As a public speaker she is eloquent and logical, her arguments clear-cut and convincing, while she could hold the closest attention of her audience. She is a true philantropist, as, together with her family, she has assisted many a young person in furthering their education through the administering of the REBECCA DUBBS SCHOLARSHIP FUND. Her name, her life stand for all that is pure and noble.

We have tried, by the use of the illustrations, to portray the outstanding personalities and projects throughout the years. The choice names and portraits of the rank and file, of necessity omitted, far exceed in number those mentioned and all are worthy. No one will regret more than the author the absence of some faces grown dear to all of us. In some instances we could not obtain them and of course, lack of space in such a volume precluded the use of many illustrations or pictures. With all of its inadequacies, this birdseye view of 100 years' work, with some mention of some of our outstanding national leaders, will, I feel sure, have a certain value as historic fact, and will show those outside of the ranks that at least the "grand army of reform" has not been sleeping at the switch, "but like a mighty army moved the church of God."

The facts herein written are just as the records give them, and we present them for your sincere consideration. May this record prove a fresh impetus to the work and worker. Surely the Woman's Christian Temperance Union has cause to be proud of its heritage.

MRS. FRED J. TOOZE, PRESIDENT

CONTENTS

APPENDIX

List of Illustrations

List of Illustrations (cont.)

Chapter 1

EVANSTON SUITED THE WILLARDS

The little front parlor of this historic, many-gabled house in downtown Evanston, Illinois, was crowded with city officials, WCTU officers, and many other important personages on that crisp November afternoon in 1965. They were there to place the seal of national recognition upon the 100-year-old building, not because of its age, but because it was the home of Frances Willard and the early shelter for the Woman's Christian Temperance Union which her dedication had brought into being.

From the beginning, Rest Cottage, as Frances Willard called it, was a part of the WCTU, first as her dwelling place and office, later as a shrine and museum maintained by the National organization because of its precious memories and historic background. Finally the weight of its years and the worth of its heritage placed the landmark so high in the social history of the nation that the United States government acted to give it nation-wide recognition.

Pursuing a policy of seeking out places which commemorate events and persons of outstanding importance in American history, the National Park Service of the U. S. Department of Interior had arranged with Mrs. Fred J. Tooze, President of the National WCTU, for an inspection of Rest Cottage. To qualify for registration as a National Historic Landmark, the Willard home must "possess exceptional value as commemorating or illustrating the history of the United States." [1]

The Willard House met all the requirements of the Historic Sites Survey Committee with ease. It had been associated with the lives of outstanding historic personages. It represented a great ideal espoused by a significant segment of the American people. The building and its contents had been

9

beautifully preserved with complete historic integrity. Its owners had made provision for the use of the property for purposes consistent with its historic character.

Frances Willard House was placed on the list of 608 outstanding national historic landmarks. November 19, 1965, was the day of the designation ceremony when 150 guests gathered to hear Dr. S. Sydney Bradford, National Park Service historian, Mayor John D. Emery of Evanston, Congresswoman Marguerite Stitt Church, and other notables pay tribute to Frances Willard and the Woman's Christian Temperance Union and to see Mrs. Fred J. Tooze accept the official bronze plaque presented by the U. S. Department of the Interior.[2]

It was a great day for the National WCTU, the highest recognition for a part of the organization's heritage. A recognition made possible not only by the greatness of Frances Willard but by the perceptiveness and foresight of women who, through the years, accepted the responsibility of preserving and maintaining the Willard home and its original contents as a sacred trust.

History is not made in a moment. The story of the Willard house might well reveal the history of one hundred years in the WCTU.

They Chose Evanston

Josiah Flint Willard, teacher, farmer, broker, brought his family to Evanston when it was a village of only five hundred inhabitants.

Respect for and dedication to religion and education had always been a dominant influence in the Willard home. As had their parents and grandparents before them, Josiah and Mary T. Willard invariably found their close friends and associates among "people of like mind" who "lived by the faith" and adhered rigidly to the highest moral principles. They were attracted to communities known for churches and schools rather than commercial and industrial advantages.

The Willards started their married life in a church-oriented community, the village of Churchville, New York, which had been their home since childhood. Rev. Hiram Whitcher of the Free Baptist Church has written, "Josiah Willard and Mary Hill were brought up and converted in the same society and school district with myself. I can easily account for the piety of the daughter of Joseph and Mary Willard, for no persons ever went out from our church more truly pious than were these parents." [3]

Mary Hill Willard had taught school from the time she was fifteen until her marriage at twenty-six, mostly summer school, but "I had some terms eight months long." 4

Josiah Willard's schooling had been interrupted at twenty when his father's death left him to care for his mother and the younger children and to administer the estate. In spite of responsibilities, he yearned for more schooling.

In 1841, with two children, Oliver the older, and Frances Elizabeth, who had been born in 1839, the young Willards decided to move to Oberlin, Ohio. Mr. Willard was attracted by Oberlin's reputation as a center of reform as well as of education and religion. He felt that his gifted children should have the "very best intellectual and moral surroundings." 5 He hoped that he might be able to study Latin and Greek, possibly enroll in some college courses. The Willards spent five happy years in Oberlin before the doctor advised an outdoor life as the most healthful for Mr. Willard's weak lungs.

For the next twelve years, the Willards lived in newly settled Wisconsin, a pioneer existence out of reach of school and church. Formal schooling was meager, classes taught by Mrs. Willard or by guests who occasionally made lengthy visits. Parents, as well as the children, Oliver, Frances and Mary, loved Forest Home near Janesville but the children had grown up. To receive the schooling for which they were ready, they must leave home. Oliver had had a year in the college of Beloit, Wisconsin, and the daughters a term at a college for girls in Milwaukee when Josiah Willard heard about Evanston, Illinois, "young Methodist suburb of Chicago", where a theological seminary, a college for young men, and another for young women were already functioning.

A trip to Evanston confirmed Josiah Willard's belief that it was a community with a future. Its three institutions of higher learning, each with a small building of its own, were already functioning in spite of extensive stretches of swamp land in the center of the settlement. In March, 1858, Mr. Willard took his daughters to Evanston and enrolled them in Northwestern Female College.

Men of Vision

Plans for Northwestern University had originated in the late spring of 1850 when a small group of leading ministers and earnest Christian laymen

The Josiah Willard Family

13

got together in Chicago. The preamble to the resolutions they adopted read, "The interests of sanctified learning require the immediate establishing of a university in the northwest.[6]

It was assumed that the undertaking would start with a preparatory school, located in Chicago where there were no preparatory schools of any kind, not even high schools. A Committee was appointed to search for a suitable site, another to draft a charter, and still another "to ascertain what amount can be obtained for erection and endowment." [7]

Subsequently, annual meetings were held. Sentiment for abandoning the idea of a preparatory school and forging ahead to establish a university proper gained support. Several members of the group seriously questioned the desirability of a Chicago campus. They advocated seeking a site farther north along the lake shore. That, too, presented difficulties.

Orrington Lunt, a member of the original committee and consistent supporter and promoter of Northwestern University and the Garrett Biblical Institute throughout his life, reported many years later on what happened.

> "The executive committee were always favorably inclined to go north of the city, to some point on the lake shore, for a location. There was no railroad built at that time, but one was being surveyed—the Chicago & Milwaukee. The committee made several trips, as far north as Lake Forest, but all seemed too far from the city, excepting Winnetka, which was satisfactory; but on trying, we found the site could not be bought at any such price as we could afford, being owned by several parties. It will be remembered that in going north, the travel was over what is now the Ridge road; between that and Chicago Avenue there was a wet, almost impassable slough or swamp, and so, in going north, we passed by the lake shore part, without knowing there was any suitable ground for our purpose.

> "After several trips we gave up the idea of finding a suitable place on the lake shore at the price we could afford. The committee then went out to Jefferson, west of the city, where we obtained options for the purchase of John Gray's land and other farms on the ridge, and were about to close the trade. But I had such a strong prejudice in favor of the lake shore,

14

that I could hardly give it up. I one day embraced the opportunity to come again to this locality with a friend, and while he was engaged in his business, I took a stroll over to the shore, through the wet land; I well remember walking over logs or planks on a portion of it. In looking south, it was wet and swampy. Looking north, I noticed the large oak forest trees. The thought first struck me that here was where the high and dry ground began! I wanted to look at it, but it was so near night that I gave it up; but on the way back, I began to think possibly this might be the place we were seeking for. It continued in my dreams all that night, and I could not rid myself of the fairy visions constantly pressing themselves upon my thoughts,—fanciful, beauteous pictures of the gentle, waving lake, its pebbly shore and its beautiful bluffs. These impressions settled it in my mind that I would not vote to accept the options for Jefferson, until the committee should make another trip north. They were to meet that morning, to close the trade. In accordance with my request, the matter was laid over, and a number of the committee went to examine the property. It was a pleasant August day. We drove into what is the present campus, and it was in its natural condition just as beautiful as now. We were delighted and some of the brethren threw up their hats, shouting, 'This is the place!' " [8]

The owner of the tract which the committee chose with such enthusiasm was not eager to sell. He said the land was worth fifteen or twenty dollars an acre, but offered to take several times that amount, $25,000 for the approximately 350 acres. His offer was accepted. Although Northwestern later acquired additional land by gift and purchase, the original acreage became the site of the village of Evanston. It was laid out and platted in the winter of 1853-54 by a University agent who was authorized to sell lots for one/fifth down, the balance due in five annual payments.

The dedicated university committee continued to meet. Busy Christian men devoted their time, talent, and money to the project. Fund raising required major attention. Potential "professors" were interviewed, a charter adopted.

Significant in that charter, both to Evanston and the Willards, as well as to the house designated as a National Historic Landmark more than 100

15

years later, was the paragraph which read, "No spirituous, vinous, or fermented liquors shall be sold under license or otherwise, within four miles of the location of said University, except for medicinal, mechanical, and sacramental purposes, under penalty of twenty-five dollars for each offense, to be recovered before any Justice of Peace of said County of Cook." [9]

Every lot sold or leased by the University was subject to the provisions of its original charter. University trustees placed a clause in every deed of transfer, declaring a lapse of title in case intoxicants were ever vended.

"The very announcement of this fact," wrote Frances E. Willard in 1891, "was the magnet to draw hither a class of people who were total abstainers and who desired for their children the surroundings of sobriety." [10] As soon as the village of Evanston was incorporated, an ordinance was adopted endorsing the charter requirements.

The honorable Harry L. Wells, vice president emeritus of Northwestern University, speaking before the Evanston Rotary Club, January 9, 1964, in observance of Evanston's Centennial Year, mentioned that the city of Evanston had been "molded around the thinking of a very small group of people at its best."

He agreed with Miss Willard's earlier appraisal. Said Mr. Wells, "It is no mystery why the Female College and the WCTU came to Evanston— no mystery why three private educational institutions and three seminaries came here, why the World Council of Churches met here." [11]

Wrote Miss Willard, "The muncipal officers are in hearty sympathy with the law, and although Chicago is but eleven miles away, and enforcement cannot be made perfect, it is nevertheless true, that, in the main, prohibition properly prohibits in "Evanston proper." [12] Evanston was truly the type of community which the Willards could enjoy.

A Law Tested

The dry laws of Evanston have not gone untested. Would-be saloon-keepers decided to battle them in the courts in 1880. Harvey B. Hurd, Evanston's first village board president, represented the dry side when the suit finally reached the Supreme Court. "He won a smashing victory when his opponent showed too drunk to stand, and Hurd had to present both sides of the argument." [13]

After the repeal of the 18th Amendment, an election was called for the city of Evanston on the question, "Shall the sale of alcoholic beverages be prohibited in the city of Evanston?" In the election on April 3, 1934, 11,836 Evanstonians voted for prohibition, 3,886 voted wet.[14]

In the spring of 1964, the Junior Chamber of Commerce of Evanston announced the results of an opinion poll in which 1234 citizens had responded to a similar question. More than three/fourths of those responding, 949, took a stand against the sales of alcoholic beverages in Evanston.[15]

It was not until January, 1972, that the sale of alcoholic beverages was legalized in Evanston. Refusing to call a city-wide referendum on the proposal, members of the City Council voted eleven to six to license the sale of liquor in Evanston clubs, hotels and restaurants.[16]

Mayor Edgar Vanneman, Jr. pointed out that license fees would be high and forecast that the number of licenses would probably be few. His statement, "The purpose of the bill is not to make liquor easier to obtain in Evanston, but to help downtown Evanston", [17] was indicative of the specious reasoning behind the action. By year's end, fourteen licenses to sell liquor-by-the-drink had been issued by Evanston authorities.

The House That Josiah Built

By the fall of 1858, Josiah Willard was building a home near the lake shore, a "rather better than average" residence in which the family of five delighted until the death of the younger daughter and the marriage of the son in 1862. After that, the house was too empty of dear ones, too full of memories. Josiah Willard sold it and got ready to build again.

His choice of location amazed everyone. On the west side of Chicago Avenue, in the second block south of the Northwestern campus, it was an area in which no other resident had yet ventured to build. Mr. Willard acquired the entire block.

His elder daughter, thirty years later wrote, "The ground north of Church Street, Evanston, and west of Chicago Avenue was a marsh, standing for months of the year partially under water. It was considered unhealthy and the newcomers built along the lake shore and on the west ridge. But my father was an enterprising man. He always liked to branch out and do what other people told him could not be done. So he cast a lingering eye on this moist square, leased it of the University for ninety-nine years and proceeded to drain and make it habitable.

The House Built by Josiah Willard at 1730 Chicago Avenue

"He joined with others in giving one of the lots to Mrs. Bragdon, who was the widow of our beloved pastor, and they built a comfortable home just south of us. Father sold the ground north of us to his loved friend, Professor Hemenway of Garrett Biblical Institute, and built for himself on the south half of what remained.

"Father planted a row of elms the whole length of the block and they are probably the handsomest row in town. He filled the front yard with choice and fragrant shurbs, covered the house with vines, and in two years it was one of the loveliest places in Evanston. The back yard was a pleasant pasture for our old horse, Jack.

"We moved into this house, mother thinks, on the 23rd of December, 1865, at least, it was very near Christmas time." [18]

Josiah Willard lived to enjoy his home only a few years. Northwestern University gave a quit claim deed to the property to Mary T. Willard, May 15, 1872, Lots 16 and 17 and the south ⅔ of Lot 18, Block 15, Evanston.

After Oliver Willard's death in 1878, an annex for his family was added to the Willard home. Almost equal in size to the original residence, upstairs and down, the "O. Willard half" of the cottage had its own entrances, stairways, and balconies front and back, a safe, comfortable haven for Mary Bannister Willard and her four children.

Evanston suited the Willards and the Willards suited Evanston. The house which bears their name was a commodious, attractive home in 1880 with children playing in the yard and neighbors dropping in for tea.

Ninety years later it is a National Historic Landmark.

Chapter 2

A HOUSE WHICH MADE HISTORY

It seems unlikely that Josiah Willard had any premonition of the eminence which the attractive home he had built on Chicago Avenue in Evanston might attain. His illustrious daughter, Frances Elizabeth, may have had dreams presaging its distinguished future. There was no doubt in her mind that the future of that home and the future of the WCTU were synonomous.

On Miss Willard's death, February 17, 1898, the terms of her will bequeathed a life interest in the Willard home to her sister-in-law, Mary Bannister Willard, and to Anna A. Gordon, who had been her secretary and constant companion for more than twenty years. Upon the death of her legatees, her estate was to become the property of the National Woman's Christian Temperance Union.

No one was surprised at this generous bequest. The WCTU had been Frances Willard's life, her consuming interest since 1874, and she had served as national president since 1879. During Miss Willard's life the WCTU offices had occupied quarters in downtown Chicago but Rest Cottage, as Miss Willard had always called her home, had extended its hospitality to a constant stream of the great and near-great of the temperance movement from many lands. It was filled with elaborately illuminated testimonials, silken, gold-fringed banners, unique bits of china, stone, wood—all certifying to the high regard in which she was held by countless admirers.

In 1900, the National WCTU purchased Mary Willard's life interest in the north half of the cottage for $6000 and moved their headquarters into the eight rooms "so admirably adapted for office work".[1] The resident officers voted to designate the headquarters section of the cottage as The Willard.[2]

Willard House Dining Room

Willard House Sitting Room

Anna Gordon maintained, "meeting all necessary expenses," and made her home in the south section of the cottage, "all the rooms are kept in the same condition as when Miss Willard and her mother lived in the house".[3]

Every record indicates continued and increasing satisfaction with the Evanston headquarters. Twenty-six dollars and forty cents were spent for renovating furniture. A telephone, $53.65, and an electric bell, $3.05, were installed. The water tax was $12.75, the insurance, $60.00.[4]

Lillian M. N. Stevens, National WCTU president, noted in her convention address of 1903, "Evanston is known in the educational world as the seat of Northwestern University, in the business world as the abiding place of many of Chicago's leading financiers and business men, in the social world as one of the most attractive cities in the country and in the world at large as the home of Frances E. Willard; and to her home, the people come".[5]

Having the people come was a major objective of Miss Gordon and the WCTU officers. They happily made use of the office space but consistently planned to keep the original Willard rooms intact, to preserve with historic integrity the image of one who represented a great ideal. The people came, hundreds every year—a former pupil, school mate, delegations from conventions, tourists, friends from overseas. WCTU members from everywhere.

When the National WCTU in 1903 bought their official publications, *The Union Signal* and *Young Crusader,* from the association which had published them, Miss Gordon turned over the large upstairs guest room adjoining the business offices to be used as an editorial office.[6]

Rapid growth of WCTU membership and the expanding program of the organization soon demanded more space. In 1910, a two story brick building of twelve large rooms was erected in the garden at the rear of The Willard.[7] The editorial offices and publications equipment were moved into the new building. The business offices, increasingly crowded, continued in The Willard.

Ground was broken for a headquarters building on August 8, 1921. By spring of 1922 the red brick building, connected with and standing to the south of the editorial building, was ready for occupancy.[8] Spacious offices for the National officers and their secretaries with eight additional stock rooms and a third floor assembly room had been builded and equipped for less than $50,000. By unanimous agreement the offices vacated in the

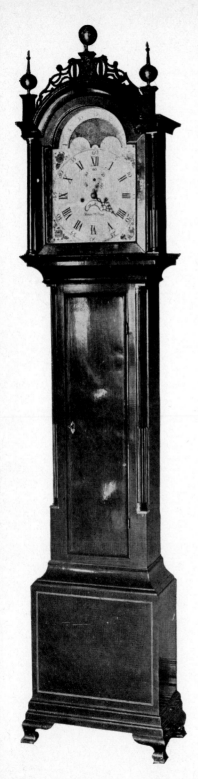

Simon Willard
Grandfather Clock
in
Willard House

Willard home were set aside to provide space for a museum.

In 1920, the Fine Arts Appraisal Company of America appraised the value of the contents of Miss Willard's den in Rest Cottage at $3000.00. Furnishings and personal effects in the other rooms added up to a total of more than $11,000.00.[9]

Some of these items, their value enhanced by years and rarity, would command fancy prices today. The signed Simon Willard tall case grandfather style clock in the Willard study is similar in appearance to the historic Willard clock which stands in the "chamber entry" of the John Quincy Adams Mansion in Massachusetts. Of polished mahogany, the carved posts edging the front panel are capped in brass and decorated with brass inserts. The brass balls surmounting the clock face housing are typical Simon Willard.[10] Constructed about 1782, the clock is equipped to record days, hours, minutes and seconds with a golden full moon peering out of the panel above the face.

Not half as handsome but of the same era is the "Wooten Secretary" in the downstairs reception room. Invented by W. S. Wooten of Indianapolis in 1874, the desk with the 99 compartments, pigeon holes and drawers is emblematic of the Victorian love for gadgetry and fine cabinet work. The beautifully preserved piece bears a silver plate engraved "Frances Willard, 1884".

The English music box, a gift to Frances Willard from Countess Somers in 1892 bears the mark of its maker, Imhof and Mukele, London. A glass panel in the inlaid wooden case permits a view of the perforated steel drums which supply the "Double Mandoline" music. After 75 years, it responds with Nearer My God to Thee, How Firm a Foundation and four additional hymns when properly handcranked. Connoisseurs say that its remarkably sweet and delicate tones are due to the fineness of the steel used in its construction.

Near the handsome mantel and hearth in Miss Willard's upstairs study is the spinning wheel which belonged to her great grandmother. Among many pictures upon the walls of this room is a portrait of a Willard ancestor, "The Reverend Mr. Samuel Willard", president of Harvard College in 1701 and for thirty years, pastor of Old South Church, Boston.[11]

Of special interest to WCTU members are such items as the yard-long bow of five-inch white satin ribbon inscribed "Ninth Street Christian Church,

YWCTU".[12] Finished with wide gold fringe, this finery is reminiscent of an auspicious occasion in President Garfield's church in Washington, D. C. The elaborately embossed pen of sterling silver used by President Wilson to sign the Eighteenth Amendment is one of several history making pens. Frances Willard's Bible, so worn that visitors may no longer turn its leaves to see the marginal notes which crowd many pages,[13] lies on her desk in her study. In the same room is the "mystery quilt" made in 1876 by the women of Ohio with a 100-year prophecy hidden in its center block.[14]

A picture of the double Willard house in Evanston in deep blue on white centers the Temperance Plate of the Methodist Historcal Tea Set. The rim of the plate, made in 1912, bears photographs of no less than six temperance landmarks, all clearly labeled and dated and including Mother Thompson's Home in Hillsboro, Ohio, the home of Lillian M. N. Stevens in Portland, Maine, and Eastnor Castle in England.

The Royal Doulton cracker jar with matching tray and cover decorated in a numbered flower pattern in shades of dark blue with rich gold tracing is in perfect condition. It and much of the other china are heirlooms of the Willard and Gordon families. A more recent acquisition is the tea service of quadruple silver plate elaborately appliqued with flowers and butterflies in sterling. Made for Helen M. Brace, a Willard cousin, her name and the date are engraved on each piece. The tea service was a gift to Willard House Museum in 1917.

The deep shelves in one room of the museum are crowded with the huge muslin rolls of the famed Polygot Petition for Home Protection which requested the rulers of the governments of the world to ban the production of alcoholic beverages and opium. The sheets of paper, bearing approximately eight million signatures representing fifty languages came from all parts of the world, have been pasted on 2000 yards of white muslin bound in red and blue. The Petition, first world-wide proclamation against alcohol and other narcotics, is credited with arousing the public conscience to recognition of the possible need for international narcotics control.[15] Launched in 1884, the Petition was displayed at the International Temperance Congress in Antwerp in 1885 and presented for the inspection of President Grover Cleveland at the White House in 1895. Exhibited at many meetings in many lands and put on display at numerous colleges,[16] it was brought back to the western continent in 1897. A project of the World's WCTU, the distinctive petition has a permanent home in Willard House.

*Madame Willard at Flax Wheel
in Willard House Study*

The drably bound volumes which fill the bookshelves in the Willard parlor entice the reader of today as they did those of a century ago. In excellent condition is Henry Trumbull's "History of the Discovery of America, of the Landing of Our Forefathers at Plymout and of their Most Remarkable Engagements with the Indians". Illustrated in color, its 256 pages were published by George Clark of Boston in 1831. A nine volume set of "The Modern Traveller" with its maps and "popular description" of the "various countries of the globe" was published in 1830.

Beautifully preserved is the bound volume of "Godey's Lady's Book", January to June, 1859. Edited, from 1837 to 1877, by Sarah Josepha Hale, crusader for equal education for boys and girls, the magazine was more than a fashion book.[17] It profuse illustrations of morning wrappers and head dresses attract less than its original contributions by Oliver Wendell Holmes and Nathaniel Hawthorne.

Among the books by authors who continue to be widely read are the well-known "Timothy's Quest" by Kate Douglas Wiggin and "Villette" by Charlotte Bronte, both published in 1891. "Beautiful Joe", the dog story by Marshall Saunders, 1893, is found in many libraries today.

Visitors to Evanston place Willard House on their list of "things to see". The mother of one bewildered family, searching for this landmark, called out, "That must be it. See the lace curtains!"

The lace curtains, stiffly white, grace the windows of the Willard rooms, as like those of 1865 as can be obtained. Flowered wall to wall carpeting approximates in design that laid by Madame Willard. The polished newell posts and stair rails are the originals as are the white marble mantel, the light fixtures, the picture frames.

The gabled exterior in grey board and batten siding with white trim and carefully preserved Victorian fret work is completely authentic. Stately elms still line the street in front of the quaint 17-room cottage. At the rear, twin chestnut trees, planted by Miss Willard, tower above Willard House and the three-story headquarters building.

The People Come

"On the occasion of the state educational meeting in Chicago a few weeks ago nearly two hundred teachers came to see the Willard home," wrote Lillian M. N. Stevens in her president's report of 1904. Through

British Friends Taught Miss Willard to Ride the Bicycle in 1893

seventy-five years they have continued to come, teachers, researchers, tourists and townspeople.

Selected groups of pupils from each of the grade schools in Evanston visited the Willard House each day during the centennial observance of Frances Willard's birthday in 1939.[18]

Seventy-four visitors from all around the world toured "Rest Cottage" during the first ten days of the meeting of the World's Council of Churches in Evanston in September of 1954. Amateur photographers could be observed aiming their kodaks at the WCTU buildings every sunshiny hour.[19]

The largest single group to visit this exciting museum included 450 young people from 27 states and five other countries who came on July 31, 1971, between sessions of the World WCTU's 25th Triennial Convention in downtown Chicago. They were followed the next day by 300 delegates from the same convention.

In 1955 Willard House underwent extensive renovation. Workmen raised sagging supports several inches, inserted steel beams and new foundations to compensate for the weight of ninety years and several long unused brick chimneys.[20] Steam heat has replaced wood stoves and fireplace heat. New plumbing and cemented basement storage have been added.

After the kitchen at Willard House had been enlarged and modernized in 1957, an invitation was extended to women's civic and religious groups to hold their meetings in the House. Many have accepted, including a tour of the museum in their programs.[21]

In 1960, Evanston Garden Clubs selected Willard House as one of the six historical homes to be featured in their Garden Fair. A jar of snap-dragons complimented the amber, gold and white lusterware shade on the brass kerosene lamp as both stood on a marble-topped table in the Willard sitting room. A huge arrangement of lilics and peonies filled the washbowl in Frances Willard's bedroom. Six hundred visitors toured the museum that week.[22]

Among recent visitors were Mrs. Mary Willard Baer of Chicago and Mrs. Robert Andrews of Carlisle, Pennsylvania, great-great nieces of Frances Willard.[23]

The historic landmark was a major attraction of the Evanston Centennial celebration in July, 1963. Its photograph dominated a page devoted to the

UNITED STATES DEPARTMENT OF THE INTERIOR
WASHINGTON, D. C.

Frances Willard House

Illinois

is hereby designated a

REGISTERED NATIONAL HISTORIC LANDMARK

Under the Provisions of the
Historic Sites Act of August 21, 1935,
This Site Possesses Exceptional Value in
Commemorating and Illustrating the
History of the United States of America.

Secretary of the Interior

Director, National Park Service

National Historic Landmark Official Designation

National WCTU in the Centennial brochure. It is one of the four Evanston buildings featured on the blue and white Centennial souvenir tile.[24]

Nation-wide recognition came to the home of Frances E. Willard officially in 1965, when a representative of the U. S. Department of the Interior presented the bronze plaque now attached to the front of the building. The Plaque reads,

> "Frances Willard House
> has been designated a
> Registered National
> Historic Landmark"

A distinction of this sort had been accorded to only 608 United States sites associated with outstanding historic personages. The National WCTU in accepting registration agreed to preserve the historic integrity of the building, to use the property in a manner consistent with its historic character and to permit periodic inspections by a representative of the National Park Service.[25]

The new national status of the Willard home, added to its heritage of purpose and dedication, has enormously expanded its potential. The casual sightseer may be attracted by Josiah Willard's plush top hat worn when he attended the May 18, 1860, meeting in Chicago's Wigwam at which Abraham Lincoln was nominated for the presidency.[26] A tourist's child may remember only the bicycle which Miss Willard learned to ride at Eastnor Castle[27] in 1892 or the nodding heads of the dainty pair of Dresden figurines on the mantel in her study.

All are a part of the history of the temperance movement, of the first one hundred years of the National Woman's Christian Temperance Union.

Chapter 3

POWERED BY PRAYER

The Women's Temperance Crusade of 1873 was a crusade of prayer. It began almost simultaneously in three separate communities in which a popular lyceum lecturer had told the same dramatic story of his drinking father and praying mother.

Speaking in Fredonia, New York, on December 14, 1873, in Hillsboro, Ohio, on December 23 and in Washington Court House, Ohio, on December 24, Dr. Dio Lewis told of his vivid memories of a childhood home impoverished by drink. He recalled that his mother, Delecta Barbour Lewis, had frequently importuned the keeper of the only saloon in Clarksville, N. Y. to refuse to sell liquor to her husband.[1] Without result. At length, Mrs. Lewis was joined by other women of the town. Day after day with Bibles in hand, they visited the local saloon where they knelt to pray. Their petitions were for the saloonkeeper to close his business and for the young mill workers of the town who were tempted by his open saloon. Their persistent prayer caused the saloon to be closed. In his lecture, Dr. Lewis was able to say, "More than forty years have passed and that town is free from saloons." [2]

The time was right for the spark which Dr. Dio's story generated. Drunkenness was widespread among men who had acquired a taste for liquor during the hardship and suffering of long service in the Civil War. Drinking, formerly considered a problem of the poor, had become a burden in homes of wealth. A tide of antagonism against the liquor traffic was rising.

In Fredonia, a "deep, strong passion" pervaded the audience after Dr.

Lewis had spoken. One hundred women rose to their feet in response to his call for women who would organize against the sale of liquor.[3]

A week later the story of Delecta Lewis's prayerful effort electrified the women of Hillsboro and Washington Court House, both in Ohio. "Sixty men agreed to act as backers of the work in Hillsboro".[4]

The pattern of the Crusade was similar in each community. Women gathered for prayer in a local church, chose leaders and walked in a group to a saloon, often singing as they went. If permitted to enter, they held a prayer meeting before the bar and often handed the bartender a petition to "earnestly request that you pledge yourself to cease the traffic here in these drinks forthwith and forever."[5]

Frances Willard described the only Crusade visit in which she had opportunity to participate. "There stood women of undoubted religious devotion and the highest character, most of them crowned with the glory of gray hairs. . . . The tall, stately lady who led us placed her Bible on the bar and read a Pslam. . . . Then we sang 'Rock of Ages' as I thought I had never heard it sung before . . . then one of the women whispered that the leader wished to know if I would pray . . . I felt not the least reluctant, and kneeling on that sawdust floor, with a group of earnest hearts around me, and behind them, filling every corner and extending out into the street, a crowd of unwashed, unkempt, hardlooking, drinking men. I was conscious that perhaps never in my life, save beside my sister Mary's dying bed, had I prayed as truly as I did then. This was my Crusade baptism."[6]

During the early months of 1874, the Women's Temperance Crusade spread over a broad area into scores of communities. Thousands of saloons closed at least temporarily. No statistics on actual results are available but interest in the movement was so general that 8000 newspapers devoted a column weekly to the temperance cause.[7]

The March 14, 1874, issue of *Harper's Weekly* profusely illustrated an article with drawings by C. S. Reinhart showing the Crusaders as they marched and prayed. *The New York Tribune* of the same date said, "A comparison of the returns of internal revenue collections in two of the largest liquor districts in Indiana and Ohio, for the months of January and February, gives some idea of the effects of the woman's temperance movement upon the liquor traffic. The total decrease in the two districts named is $353,720.14. It is estimated by revenue officers that 80 per cent

Women's Temperance Crusade, 1873

of the collections are derived from alcohol; and malt liquors; the decrease
of revenue on liquors, therefore is $282,976.12". [8]

On February 24, 1874, Dio Lewis wrote of his elation at the impact of
"one of my long-cherished ideas."

"The world has seen nothing like this woman's temperance movement.
Religious revivals are often characterized by wild extravagance. These
saloon meetings are marked by all the quiet dignity and deep solemnity of
family devotions. Thousands unaccustomed to religious thought exclaim;
'This is of God!' It is sweeping over the country like a magnificent prairie
fire." [9]

The most significant result of the Crusade was the awakening of women
of substantial background to the universal threat of the liquor traffic. Women,
whose sheltered lives and abstaining families had made them indifferent to
the harm caused by drinking, were aroused to the need to become involved.
The Women's Temperance Crusade provided a dramatic demonstration of
the effectiveness of selfless prayer and earnest dedication. The duration of
the Crusade proper was scarcely more than six months but it inspired a
consciousness which soon took concrete form in organization.

Organize for Orderly Procedure

Praying bands in many communities recognized the enormity of the task
they had undertaken. They felt a need to define their objective in print,
to elect officers, to husband their resources by orderly procedure.

At the end of their first week, the Crusaders in Fredonia, N. Y. adopted
a pledge. "We, the undersigned women of Fredonia, feeling that God has
lain upon us a work to do for temperance, do hereby pledge ourselves
to united and continuous effort to suppress the traffic in intoxicating liquors
in our village until this work be accomplished; and that we will stand
ready for united effort upon any renewal of the traffic. We will also do
what we can to alleviate the woes of drunkards' families, and to rescue
from drunkenness those who are pursuing its ways. This society shall be
known as the Woman's Temperance Union of Fredonia." [10]

A few days later women in Jamestown, N.Y. organized "The Ladies'
Temperance Society, Auxiliary to the Jamestown Total Abstinence Society." [11] On February 24, 1874, the first "state" convention of the women's
temperance movement met in City Hall of Columbus, Ohio. According to

Frances E. Willard
National President 1879-1898

local historians, the organization initiated there became the Ohio WCTU a few months later.[12] By fall Indiana had a "state" organization in complete working order, with plans for a central organization in every township.[13]

Christian women throughout the nation felt the urge to participate. The story of women overcoming evil by unified patience, persistence and prayer challenged the imagination.

So it was that three such women, Mrs. Jennie Fowler Willing, Illinois Weslyan University faculty member; Mrs. Emily Huntington Miller, juvenile fiction writer of Evanston, Illinois, and Mrs. Mattie McClellan Brown of Ohio, a leader in Good Templar work, took the initiative.

They, with interested women from a dozen other states, were attending the National Sunday School Assembly at Chautauqua Lake, New York, in August of 1874. Encouraged by the Assembly leadership, they held several temperance meetings during the sessions and finally named an eleven-member Committee of Organization from among themselves and called for a National organizing convention to convene in Cleveland, Ohio, in November, 1874. The response was encouraging; 135 women from 17 states gathered on November 18, in the Second Presbyterian Church in Cleveland.[13]

They came because they realized that any attempt to cope with the evils caused by drink must go beyond the temporary measures of converting saloonkeepers and reforming drunkards. Dedicated to the protection of homes, powered by prayer, they quietly accepted the liquor traffic as their adversary and set about forming an organization which would stand against a "common danger" and follow a "common hope" for more than 100 years.

As temporary chairman, Mrs. Jennie Fowler Willing, Bloomington, Illinois, expressed their sentiments. "You have no need to be reminded that this is simply and only a religious movement. If this convention carries strongly the interests committed to it, it will be simply because we are lost to ourselves in a devotion to our work. Many are praying for us. Noble men of the nation, women delicate and earnest, women hidden in poverty and obscurity, are all praying for us. There is not a woman here who shrinks from the duties of this hour, because we are strong in Him who says, "And if any man lack wisdom, let him ask of God who giveth to all men liberally and upbraideth not." [14]

That was the spirit which pervaded the convention, "Strong in Him!" Women had come together to undertake an uncharted course. They were

The Willard Window
National WCTU Headquarters

not sure of themselves but they were sure that widespread sale and use of alcoholic beverages were a scourge in the land. With selfless dedication, they sought to know and be directed by God's will. The organization which resulted was characterized seventy-five years later as "the matchless machine manned by Christian women and powered by prayer." [15]

The organizing convention had been called for the express purpose of welding into a nation-wide force the temperance groups which were already functioning in several states. Plans and policies must be adopted which would encourage local initiative and effort but direct it toward a common objective.

A name was chosen—Woman's Christian Temperance Union, a name unchanged through 100 years. Consistency—"if nobody would drink, then nobody would sell"—dictated a total abstinence pledge as a basis for membership. Officers were elected.

Looking back on the organizing convention Frances Willard wrote in 1876, "A phenomenon no less remarkable, though certainly much less remarked, succeeded the crusade—indeed, is aptly termed its "sober second thought." This was the phenomenon of *organization*. The women who went forth by an impulse, sudden, irresistible, divine, to pray in the saloons, became convinced, as weeks and months passed by, that theirs was to be no easily-won victory. The enemy was rich beyond their power to comprehend. He had upon his side the majesty of law, the trickery of politics, and the leagued strength of that almost invincible pair—appetite and avarice. He was persistent, too, as fate; determined to fight it out on that line to the last dollar of his enormous treasure-house and the last ounce of his power. But these women of the crusade believed in God, and in themselves as among his appointed instruments to destroy the rum-power in America. They loved Christ's cause, they loved the native land that had been so mindful of them; they loved their sweet and sacred homes; and so it came about that, though they had gone forth only as skirmishers, they soon fell into line of battle; though they had ignorantly hoped to take the enemy by a sudden assault, they buckled on the armor for the long campaign. The Women's Praying Bands, earnest, impetuous, inspired, became the Woman's Temperance Unions, firm, patient, perservering. The Praying Bands were without leadership, save that which inevitably results from "survival of the fittest"; the Woman's Unions are officered in the usual way. Enthusiasm—a "God in us"—enabled the Praying Bands to accomplish prodigies; steady purpose, and

National Leadership Training School, 1966

the same faith which inspired the crusade, is conducting the Unions to victory, distant, but sure." [16]

From the first a major emphasis of the WCTU was on membership, organization, leadership. One of the early standing committees was "On Plans for Interesting and Enlisting More Workers."

Nationally elected officers were expected to seek opportunities to speak publicly for the cause, to enroll new members and effect local and state organizations. In 1876, Mrs. Annie T. Wittenmyer, National president, and Mrs. Mary R. Denman, president of New Jersey WCTU, made organizing trips to Kentucky, Tennessee and Louisiana. Mrs. Wittenmyer visited Washington in 1878 and organized the District of Columbia union.

The years 1882 and 1883 were the great organizing years in the history of the Woman's Christian Temperance Union. During those years, Frances E. Willard, National president, and Anna Adams Gordon, her secretary, traveled almost 30,000 miles. Setting out with the ambition to speak in every city with a population of 10,000 or more, they were able to report at the November 3, 1883 convention that every state and territory had been organized with regularly elected officers.

But "those were the days when a temperance meeting, especially a temperance meeting addressed by a woman, demanded and found an audience." [17] Speakers seemed to spring up spontaneously. By 1886, the National WCTU listed as available, eleven field workers, eight organizers and three lecturers. Many more were speaking and organizing in their own states.

Mrs. Stevens and Miss Gordon traveling for about nine weeks in 1905 tied ninety yards of white ribbon into bows for new members. [18] The net gain in membership for 1915 announced at the National Convention was 29,711. [19]

At the same time, a department of work known as "School of Methods" or "WCTU Institutes" was adopted, recommended for each local and state organization as well as the National WCTU. In 1891 a National WCTU Training School of six weeks duration was undertaken to develop trained workers. In 1924, the Jubilee Year, fifty national-state meetings were held with six National leaders in each. The leaders alone traveled 52,821 miles. [20]

By the late 1930's field work had greatly diminished. Only four organizers were listed. National had few speakers to offer and they were not

CORRESPONDING SECRETARIES, 1874-1949

Mrs. Caroline B. Buell
1880-1893

Frances E. Willard
1874-1877

Mrs. Mary T. Burt
1877-1880

Mrs. Susanna M. D. Fry
1898-1908

Mrs. Katherine Lente
Stevenson
1894-1898

Mrs. Frances Pride
Parks
1908-1927

Mrs. Anna Marden
DeYo
1927-1942

Miss Lily Grace
Matheson
1942-1948

Miss Elizabeth A. Smart
1948-1950

Mrs. Mary Woodridge, 1893-1894

CORRESPONDING SECRETARIES

1950-1973

Mrs. H. R. Runion
1950-1952

Mrs. H. E. Mielke
1952-1956

Mrs. Fred J. Tooze
1956-1959

Mrs. Herman Stanley
1959-

in demand. Plans in the Organization Department called for grants to be made to state WCTU's who would use the money to finance local workers.

In 1944, Miss Lily Grace Matheson, Corresponding Secretary of the National WCTU, conducted a Leadership Training School "to develop organizers and to give WCTU workers a better understanding of the program of the organization." So encouraging was the response that a two-week training course at National Headquarters became an annual event. In 1954, Mrs. H. E. Mielke was able to report "Seventy-six registrants from thirty-two states were in the school this year." [21] In 1971, twelve states held their own Leadership training Schools.

Early leaders in the WCTU adopted a Declaration of Principles so inclusive that it has guided the policy and program of the organization through one hundred years. Later leaders have been wise enough to emphasize the basic purpose while adjusting means and methods to meet current conditions.

At the third convention, definite plans were made for the observance of special WCTU days at summer resort areas such as Old Orchard Beach, Maine; Ocean Grove, N. J. and Chautauqua, N. Y. In 1876, camp meetings and summer assemblies were drawing whole families of vacationers to such attractive spots. Railroads offered excursion rates for travelers. Religious and educational organizations of all types established headquarters on the grounds, brought in speakers, conducted study courses.

Hundreds of such assemblies were held in the various states. WCTU participation was a major project of the state organizations for forty years. WCTU women found kindred spirits and favorable opportunities for presenting their program. Many state WCTU's built their own cottages on the assembly grounds, brought in speakers of renown and were recognized as adding prestige to the assembly.

The National WCTU maintained a headquarters building at Chautauqua Assembly until 1946. Originally the WCTU had been chosen as one of the educational organizations elected to share in the Anne Kellogg Building erected in 1882. A stained glass window, honoring the memory of Frances E. Willard, was installed in that building[22] and removed to Frances Willard House which the WCTU purchased on the Chautauqua grounds in 1924.[23] When this building was sold, the beautiful window was brought to Evanston. Since 1957 it has graced the downstairs lobby of the Headquarters Building.

WCTU Day is still a part of the Summer Assembly at Chautauqua with a National WCTU officer directing the program and greeting busloads of WCTU members who come from surrounding areas. Among the many prominent speakers who have headlined the day's program are Judge Joseph T. Zottoli, Boston; H. Cecil Heath, London; Dr. Andrew C. Ivy, former vice president of University of Illinois professional schools; Dr. Carl S. Winters, staff lecturer for General Motors; Mrs. Masako Munakata, president of the WCTU of Japan, Tokyo; Dr. Joy Elmer Morgan, editor of NEA Journal.

The eagerness of the women in the early conventions resulted in an almost endless list of committees for department work. Appointed in 1879 were committees On Inducing Corporations and Employers to Require Total Abstinence in Their Employees, Temperance Restaurants and Reading Rooms, On Unfermented Wine, Sabbath Desecration, Work Among Sailors, and twenty others. Many of these continued until their objectives had been accomplished or were taken over by organizations devoted to that specific purpose. Many public libraries had their beginnings in the temperance reading rooms. Several organizations devote their attention to Sabbath observance.

Many departments were dropped as time went on or replaced by others more appropriate. In 1890 a School Savings Bank Department undertook to interest schools and bankers in teaching thrift to school children. This effort was taken over wholeheartedly by the banks and schools. Department work by WCTU women is generally conceded to have caused police matrons to be added to prison staffs, to have hastened the adoption of the Pure Food and Drugs Act, and to have banned the sending of liquor through the mails.

All through the years departments have functioned to carry on the educational, charitable and legislative activities of the WCTU. What was once Scientific Temperance Instruction is now Narcotic Education. Temperance & Missions has become Christian Outreach.

Until National Prohibition was adopted in 1920, almost no fruit juices, except grape juice, were bottled. With characteristic alertness, the WCTU began to publish recipes for fruit punches and milk drinks. In 1929, the Department of Non-alcoholic Fruit Products was originated to promote the social use of non-alcoholic beverages. The department name was changed to Natural Fruit Beverages in 1950 and is now merged with other

45

National WCTU Headquarters

Projection Methods, but the successful effort to glamorize non-alcoholic beverages continues unabated.

World Wide Interest

Even though the world-wide satellite communication system of the 1970's was not available, the story of the Women's Temperance Crusade of 1873 spread into the English speaking countries of the world. The report of women organizing to protect their homes from alcoholic liquor aroused interest and hope in concerned women everywhere.

Mrs. Letitia Youmans of Canada came to the Second National WCTU Convention in Cincinnati to learn first hand what might be done by Canadian women. Early in 1876, Mother Stewart, member of the first Crusading band at Hillsboro, Ohio, accepted an invitation from the temperance forces of Great Britain. She and Mrs. Mary C. Johnson spent six months in an almost uninterrupted schedule of meetings in the British Isles. Before they left, the British Women's Temperance Association had been organized.

The National WCTU hosted an International Temperance Convention of women in Philadelphia in 1876. Delegates came from nearly every state as well as from Canada, Great Britain and Japan, but no organization resulted.

The national officers announced at their 1883 convention in Detroit that they were formulating plans for the organization of a World's WCTU. At St. Louis the next year, Miss Willard reported, "Letters have been sent out to the leading missionaries of Christendom asking their advice and cooperation as to the best methods of initiating this great enterprise." [24]

The Polyglot Petition for Home Protection, originated by Francis Willard, and launched at the Philadelphia convention in 1885 was the unifying force which drew the women of the World together to pursue a common objective. Addressed to the rulers of all countries, it urged them "to strip away all safeguards" which legalized "the drink traffic and opium trade."

For the next five or six years the petition was received with enthusiasm the world around. Mrs. Mary Clement Leavitt carried it into the Sandwich Islands and New Zealand where she also organized local and provincial unions of the WCTU. Other workers were in Australia, India, South Africa and Japan. As the list of signatures on the petitions lengthened, WCTU organizations spread into many nations.

47

Pursuing the objective of World organization, leaders in the USA, Great Britain, Canada, Wales and Australia by correspondence selected Mrs. Margaret Bright Lucas of London, sister of John Bright, great English Commoner, as first World president in 1885. No formal meeting was held until 1891, when a World's organizing convention met in Boston preceding the 18th National WCTU Convention in the same city. Fifteen countries were represented. Officers were elected, constitution and by-laws adopted.

Again in 1893, the second World's convention was held in conjunction with the United States Convention at Chicago. But World delegates assembled in London in 1895 and have met since in all parts of the world, Edinburgh, New Delhi, Toronto, Geneva, Mexico City, Washington, D.C., Bremen, Tokyo. The latest convention at Chicago in 1971, with Mrs. T. Roy Jarrett of Virginia presiding, attracted 1500 people representing thirty-six countries. Australia and Japan each sent sixteen delegates. Twenty-one came from England, twenty-eight from Canada and hundreds from all over the United States.

The Woman's Christian Temperance Union is truly a world-wide organization with some type of organization today in each of 72 different countries. Although a desire and purpose to combat the evil of alcohol and other narcotic drugs is the basic philosophy which undergirds the WCTU organizations everywhere, the emphasis varies widely among the nations. Clinics for narcotics addicts have been sponsored in Finland. Japan has been instrumental in building a home for mothers and children. The Danish union operates a residence hotel for the elderly. Australia and Canada have been significantly successful in the promotion of soft drinks as substitutes for alcoholic beverages. Opium and heroin are a deeper concern than alcohol in some countries. Rehabilitation of alcoholics received major attention in others. Prevention through education is the emphasis in several countries as it is in the USA.

Although their eyes were bright with purpose and their prayers were filled with faith, the Women of the Temperance Crusade could not have envisioned the scope of the movement they started, the multiplicity of the facets, the complexity of its functioning. Accomplishments have been many, disappointments deep.

On the 50th anniversary of the Crusade, December 23, 1923, WCTU women sang and prayed as they traversed the route of the first praying band in Hillsboro. They were lead by the mayor and accompanied by two hundred men and women of like mind. Not one saloon stood on their route. National Prohibition was in its third year.

By 1974 the liquor traffic in the United States threatened the welfare of the nation and its citizens as it had one hundred years before. It posed a problem overwhelming except to those powered by prayer.

1968 World's Convention in Tokyo

Chapter 4

LIQUOR AND LAW

The need for legislation in any attempt to deal with the liquor traffic was recognized by the Woman's Christian Temperance Union at their very first meeting. The newly elected officers of the infant organization were directed by a vote of those in session to prepare and present a Memorial to Congress.

Mrs. Annie T. Wittenmyer, first president of the National WCTU, assumed responsibility. Ten thousand copies of the prepared petition called upon the Congress to note "the destruction which the use of alcoholic liquors is inflicting upon the American people" and after thorough investigation "to report the same to aid in intelligent and efficient action." [1]

At the next convention Mrs. Wittenmyer reported that copies of petitions sent out over the nation had been returned so promptly and in such numbers that counting of signatures had been discontinued at 40,000. After that they were simply marked "uncounted thousands", pasted on yards of muslin which made a "roll as big as a sheep" and taken to Washington in early February of 1875. [2]

By 1877, President Wittenmyer was recommending a new and stronger memorial for presentation to the 1879 session of Congress, a memorial which "may be the largest ever laid before an official body." Mrs. Wittenmyer's suggestion, "I would like to see in that petition a clause asking for the disenfranchisement of the habitual drunkard. This will strip the liquor dealers of their mightiest weapons in politics", showed that the women of the WCTU were aware of the enormity of their task. [3]

Neither the liquor problem nor recognition of alcohol's pernicious effects were new when the WCTU was organized.

Liquor has been a social problem for at least 4000 years. Every nation and every generation has been plagued by the use of alcohol as a beverage. In the fifth century, B.C., Plato wrote, "I should prefer a law to the effect that nobody while on military duty must ever taste this drink, but must keep entirely to water . . . that in the city no slave taste wine at any time, nor the President during his year of presidency . . . nor the judges while on duty." [4]

The use of alcoholic beverages was common in Colonial America.[5] Drunkenness was a factor in Indian raids and massacres.[6] Among the earliest liquor laws were those prohibiting the sale of whisky to slaves or apprentices.

In 1785, Dr. Benjamin Rush of Philadelphia, a signer of the Declaration of Independence, published his historic essay, *The Effects of Ardent Spirits upon the Human Mind and Body.* Its conclusion, "Thus we see poverty and misery, crimes and infamy, disease and death, are all natural and usual consequences of the intemperate use of ardent spirits." [7]

The saloon became a constant public demonstration of the evils associated with the consumption of alcoholic beverages. Civic leaders reacted accordingly. In 1826 Lyman Beecher published six powerful sermons on intemperance and the American Temperance Society was organized.

In 1847 the United States Supreme Court definitely established the right of the states to exercise their power to stop the traffic in intoxicating liquors. Thereafter, within four years, 1851-1855, thirteen states enacted prohibition laws.[8] Public sentiment which favored abstinence grew dramatically. The spirit of the times branded both drinkers and sellers of liquor as lawless.

At this point the slavery question began to overshadow the liquor problem in the minds of the people and in the affairs of the states. The prohibition movement was temporarily brought to a halt by the Civil War. Attention was diverted to that overwhelming struggle, the effort to finance it, the recession which followed. The thirteen prohibition states dwindled to six.

In 1862, Congress passed an Internal Revenue Act imposing a tax upon alcoholic liquor. Although adopted as a means to help meet the extraordinary expenses of a nation at war, the tax, in the minds of many, had a tendency to "raise the status of liquor from a low, disreputable trade to a recognized, legitimate business." [9]

Through the century since that time, the tax revenue which can be received by nation, state and city from the legal sale of various types of alcoholic beverages has provided a safeguard of inestimable value to the liquor traffic. The liquor interests have been shrewd enough to perceive that the billions of dollars in taxes flowing from liquor sales have a tendency to entrench the business firmly into the economic pattern of the country. Any relaxation of restrictive liquor laws—which results in greater sale and consumption of alcohol—finds support because of the tangible appeal of additional revenue. Consistency indicates that intangible costs of liquor-caused troubles outweigh tax benefits, but these are difficult to document.

Drinking increased during the years of the Civil War. As it closed soldiers returning to the restraints of home life oftimes dimmed the warmth of their welcome by drunken orgies. Women of wealth saw their homes threatened by what they had formerly considered a problem of the poor. State governing bodies increasingly considered methods for curtailing and regulating the sale and consumption of liquor.

The Woman's Christian Temperance Union was not alone in feeling that national legislation was an absolute essential in any successful limitation of the sale of alcoholic beverages. The Independent Order of Good Templars with over 600,000 members in 1874 stood for "total abstinence from all intoxicating liquor as a beverage" and "absolute prohibition of their manufacture, importation and sale—prohibited by the will of the people, expressed in due form of law."

The Prohibition party had been formed in 1869, the Intercollegiate Prohibition Association in 1887. The Anti-Saloon League organized in 1893.

Every Protestant denomination in the land took a public stand for abstinence and for outlawing the traffic. Archbishop Ireland of the Catholic Church expressed the attitude of a growing number of American citizens— "We have seen there is no hope for improving in any way or form the liquor traffic; there is nothing now to be done but to wipe it out completely. The state alone can save us." [10]

As early as 1887, Senator Blair of New Hampshire introduced in the U. S. Senate a proposed amendment to the Constitution—

> "Section 1. The manufacture, importation, exportation, transportation and sale of all alcoholic liquors as a beverage shall be, and hereby is, forever prohibited in the United States and in every place subject to their jurisdiction."

**LEGISLATIVE
DIRECTORS
AT THE
WASHINGTON
OFFICE**

Mrs. Alexander Stewart
1948-1950

Mrs. Lenna Lowe Yost
1918-1930

Miss Izora Scott
1930-1940

Mrs. Margaret Dye Ellis
1895-1918

Miss Elizabeth Smart
1940-1948

Miss Elizabeth Smart
1950-1959

LEGISLATIVE REPRESENTATIVES
1959-1973

Mrs. Glenn G. Hays
1959-1962

Mrs. Mildred Harmon
1962-1972

Mrs. Marian B. Crymes
1972-

A Senate committee reported the bill favorably. The Judiciary Committee in the House reported it adversely.[11]

Organizations opposed to Prohibition were functioning also. Many of them were trade organizations who spared "neither means nor money" to protect their interests. A resolution adopted by the United States Brewers' Association in 1871 illustrates the singleness of purpose which governed their campaign. "The committee on agitation is hereby authorized and directed to select in each congressional district three brewers residing therein as a local and provisional organizing committee for such district, whose duty it shall be to organize by means best suited to the locality all the defenders of the rights of man . . . in order to defeat at all elections any candidates for office whose success might give encouragement to temperance fanatics and religious hypocrites to carry out their proposed proscriptive, injurious and dangerous plans." [12]

The WCTU was moving with the times in the last quarter of the 19th century when it repeatedly called attention to the need for Congressional action to curb the power and the growth of the liquor traffic. While giving wholehearted support to the Prohibition Party's stand for National Prohibition, the leaders of the WCTU—Frances Willard, Lillian M. N. Stevens, Anna A. Gordon—made repeated attempts to influence other political parties to include prohibition planks in their platforms. Rapidly gaining in membership and influence while promoting an extensive educational program, the WCTU not only cooperated with numerous other organizations, but led the way in seeking legislation in lesser matters related to alcoholic beverages. They asked that the sale of intoxicating liquor be banned from the grounds of the Centennial Exposition at Philadelphia, that liquor dealers be required to obtain the signatures of a majority of all residents over 18 years of age before a saloon could be opened in any community. WCTU effort to prohibit sale of liquor in military installations extended through 25 years, was rewarded in 1900 by the passage of the anti-canteen law.[13]

Legislative Office in Washington

It was not until 1895 that the National WCTU opened a legislative office in Washington, D. C. Mrs. Margaret Dye Ellis of New Jersey was in charge. The next twenty years saw a growing impatience on the part of people generally with the lawlessness of the liquor traffic, and a gradual tightening of the restrictions placed on the liquor interests resulted.

The WCTU publicly supported local option in 1906. The ever-increasing expanse of territory dry by local option, sometimes only a few city blocks, sometimes an entire state, showed the desire of the people to protect their homes from the saloon. It also showed that they were dealing with a lawless element which ignored local option boundary lines, bribed officials and thwarted the liquor ban through every possible contrivance that superior force and organization could effect. Local efforts dramatized the need for national prohibition.

In 1911, Mrs. Lillian M. N. Stevens, president of the National WCTU, made her historic prediction "within a decade, prohibition shall be placed in the Constitution of the United States." Mrs. Stevens, a native of Maine who had been vigorously involved in the campaign when the state adopted constitutional prohibition in 1884, and again in 1911 when a strenuous battle was necessary to prevent its repeal, read the signs aright.[14] From then on, every slow, painstaking milestone pointed the way to national prohibition.

In 1912 Congress passed the Webb-Kenyon Bill and the U. S. Supreme Court upheld its validity. This legislation prohibited the shipment of any alcoholic beverage into the eight states which had adopted state-wide prohibition.[15] State laws had been virtually nullified by the flood of liquor dealers had been sending by freight, mail and express.

The Christian Endeavor Society had adopted the slogan, "A Saloonless Nation by 1920." Prohibition states were broadcasting statistics which clearly demonstrated the benefits of banning legal liquor.

On February 9, 1915, the Kansas Legislature adopted Joint Resolution No. 33 labelling any report that prohibition was disadvantageous to Kansas as "libelous and false."[16] The Governor of Kansas, Walter R. Stubbs, asserted in a Chicago speech that prohibition had reduced both drunkenness and crime in Kansas while bank deposits had grown and general business conditions had improved.[17]

The Honorable H. T. Helgesen, a North Dakota Congressman, said of that state in 1912, "By wiping out in a large measure the most prolific cause of crime, it (prohibition) has lowered the cost of the administration of our criminal courts to a point scarcely equalled anywhere in the United States." [18]

Alice Hughes   52 Gower St London

Mrs. Lillian M. N. Stevens
National President 1898-1914

Officials of several southern states—Georgia, Tennessee, North Carolina —testified as to the benefits of prohibition. The *Atlanta Constitution* printed comments on the January 1, 1911, business census of that state in which leaders in every field gave state prohibition credit for unparalleled prosperity.[19] Governor Glenn said crime had diminished 50 per cent in his state, North Carolina.

Oklahomans were profuse in citing examples of the benefits of prohibition.[20] J. H. Johnson, secretary of Oklahoma City Chamber of Commerce, wrote, "In addition to being manager of the chamber of commerce, I am president of a retail furniture house, which does a large amount of installment business, and I can say to you frankly that so far as my business is concerned, it is much better than with the open saloon." [21]

The liquor dealers themselves were getting the message. More than four years before Congress voted on the proposed amendment, a statement in *National Liquor Dealers' Journal* read, "To us there is the handwriting on the wall and its interpretation spells doom. The liquor business is to blame. It seems incapable of learning any lesson of advancement or any motive but profit. To perpetuate itself it has formed alliances with the slums. . . . It deliberately aids the most corrupt political powers." [22]

National Prohibition

The prohibition amendment was adopted in December, 1917, by a Congress, the members of which had been elected in a campaign in which prohibition had been a major issue. The Senate voted for the amendment 65 to 20, the House 282 to 128. Within thirteen months it had been ratified by 36 states. In twenty-one ratifying state legislatures not a single wet vote was cast.[23] It was abundantly evident that an overwhelming majority of the people felt that the nation should be rid of the liquor traffic.

Lillian M. N. Stevens did not live to celebrate the victory to which she had contributed so much. Upon her sudden death in April, 1914, Miss Anna Adams Gordon stepped up to the presidency of the National WCTU. Five years later, Mrs. Lenna Lowe Yost of West Virginia, who had assisted Mrs. Ellis for two years, became head of the WCTU Legislative Bureau in Washington, D.C. Her regime continued until 1930.

Mrs. Yost served during the prohibition years when one would assume that the Legislative Bureau might be resting on its laurels. Such was not the case. During the year which elapsed between the ratification of the 18th Amendment and the date upon which it became effective, the liquor interests continued to manufacture and sell. Drinking people who were financially able filled their cellars and warehouses with the still legal liquor.[24] The campaign to repeal prohibition began before the law actually went into effect.

During the prohibition years citizens who observed the intensive effort being exerted to discredit the law did their best to get the truth before the people. Samuel G. Blythe, distinguished journalist, wrote for the *Saturday Evening Post* of July 9, 1927, "A new and gigantic purchasing power has developed in this country since we have had prohibition that accounts for the prosperity of our railroads, our manufacturies, our trade in all directions. That, in large measure, is a purchasing power derived from the diversion of former booze money into economic channels. It does not come from the very rich, nor from the very poor. It comes from the great average American citizen, and it comes in part because saloons are gone." [25]

In her *Give Prohibition Its Chance*, published in 1929, Dr. Ella A. Boole said, "The Wets make a great deal out of Maryland, New York, Montana, Nevada, and Wisconsin. Those states were wet states before prohibition. The Wets utilize the names of those states over and over again, completely overlooking the fact that these states are exceptions; that forty-three states have state enforcement codes and are cooperating with the Federal government in law enforcement." [26]

Throughout the prohibition years, the WCTU emphasis was on law enforcement and law observance. Each local union was asked to contribute two dollars each year to the Lillian Stevens Legislative Fund. This Fund has continued through the years to support the WCTU Bureau of Legislation in Washington.

Dr. Izora Scott was Legislative Director during the difficult years when repeal was accomplished and the liquor interests began their campaign to entrench alcohol as a beverage into the life and culture of the country. She served from 1930 to 1940.

Power of Propaganda

Fletcher Dobyns in his thoroughly documented *The Amazing Story of Repeal* (1940) presents an exhaustive survey of the conditions which re-

Michigan YTCers at WCTU Legislative Day, Lansing, Michigan, 1966

sulted in the repeal of the 18th Amendment in 1934. The subtitle of his book, "An Expose' of the Power of Propaganda", seems to indicate his basic conclusion.

Mr. Dobyns calls attention to several weaknesses in the prohibition law and its administrative statutes which made enforcement difficult. The use of the term "intoxicating liquor" instead of "alcoholic liquor" opened enforcement to endless litigation through dishonest experts and crooked lawyers. The law prohibited manufacture and sale but not the purchase and use of liquor. The exemption of the purchaser flouted justice and common sense.

Al Capone, the gang leader whose name is legend, said, "I make my money by supplying a public demand. If I break the law, my customers, who number hundreds of the best people in Chicago, are as guilty as I am. The only difference between us is that I sell and they buy. Everybody calls me a racketeer. I call myself a business man." [27]

The Volstead Act instead of being a concise, unequivocal enforcement vehicle, contained 73 sections of rules and regulations, exceptions and modifications. An involved permit system for industrial, medical, sacramental use of alcohol, all of which could well have been omitted, placed the administration of the law in the treasury department instead of entrusting it to the established enforcement agencies of the Federal government.

Any inadquacy of enforcement was grist for the propaganda mill of the repealists. Political corruption, racketeering, all crimes of violence including the kidnapping of the Lindbergh baby were blamed on prohibition. Mr. Dobyns commented "Every informed person knows that the gangster and the racketeer put in their appearance fifty years before the adoption of the Eighteenth Amendment, and that crimes of violence increased steadily during those years." [28]

A 1926 survey by the Illinois Association for Criminal Justice reported, "Organized crime is not, as many think, a recent phenomenon in Chicago. A study of vice, crime and gambling during the last 25 years shows the existence of crime and vice gangs during that period and how they have become more and more highly organized and powerful. Finally, with the coming of prohibition the personnel of organized crime took the lead in the systematic organization of this new and profitable field of exploitation." [29]

The Association Against the Prohibition Amendment, incorporated in April, 1919, declared its two immediate aims:

"(1) To prevent the country from going on a bone dry basis on July 1,

"(2) To make the Eighteenth Amendment forever inoperative." [30]

Those in control of the AAPA were largely men of prominence in political or financial circles. Some were allied directly with the liquor industry; many were not. During the prohibition years it became abundantly evident that they were committed to ignoring the Constitution, disregarding law, corrupting public officials and respecting nothing except their own selfish interests. Their final report noted, "A great debt is due to the liberal press of the nation which has been a factor of overwhelming importance in the accomplishment of repeal." [31]

After World War I in the early years of prohibition, the Federal income tax, which had been negligible, began to soar. Men of wealth were willing to invest large sums of money to bring about repeal in the expectation that revenue from the sale of legal liquor would reduce the income tax levied on corporations. Testimony before a Senate Committee in October, 1926, brought out that m. Irenee Du Pont, a heavy contributor to AAPA, was convinced that repeal would lift $10 million in corporation tax from one of his companies. [32]

Said Fletcher Dobyns in 1940, "The only people who have benefited financially from repeal have been liquor dealers, large income taxpayers, the underworld and wet politicians." [33]

The depression of the late '20's and early '30's was the tool used to assure repeal. The average citizen had neither time nor ability to analyze the complicated propaganda which "proved" that national prohibition caused the depression, even though the depression was world-wide and had come earlier and more severely in countries such as England and Germany which were not "afflicted with prohibition." They were told that repeal would reestablish a great industry, re-employ labor, bring relief to farmers, enlarge the business of the railroads, take from the backs of the people a "staggering load of taxation", balance the budget.

The election of Franklin D. Roosevelt in 1932 assured the repealists of cooperation from the White House, although the ineptness and apathy of his three predecessors had hurt rather than helped the image of prohibition.

Mrs. Ella A. Boole
NATIONAL PRESIDENT, 1925-1933

The Judiciary Committee of the Senate offered a resolution for repeal of the Eighteenth Amendment specifying that "it shall have been ratified by the legislatures of the several states as provided in the Constitution."

Ever alert, able and aware, the AAPA foresaw that it would probably be impossible to influence three-fourths of the state legislatures to ratify repeal. After all, state legislators were elected by and to represent districts within the state. It was a foregone conclusion that the elected legislators of at least thirteen states would refuse to vote for repeal.

Undaunted by the Judiciary Committee proposal, the repealists had written a resolution of their own. It provided for ratification by "conventions in the various states." Not as provided by the Constitution. They had already set up the plans for conventions in states where the wet influences deemed them necessary, conventions whose personnel would be chosen by statewide vote in which the controlled big-city vote could dominate. The AAPA had sufficient control in the Congress. The language the repealists demanded was incorporated into the Twenty-first Amendment to the Constitution. Ratification by the required number of states excised the Eighteenth Amendment, the first ever to be removed from the Constitution.

The Challenge of Repeal

Mrs. Ida B. Wise Smith of Iowa had assumed the presidency of the National WCTU just before repeal when Mrs. Boole's duties as World's WCTU president claimed all of her attention. How well Mrs. Smith, working with Miss Scott, met the legislative demands in this crucial period is graphically shown in a paragraph from the *Brewers Journal* of October 15, 1944.

"Mrs. Wise-Smith, taking up the broken threads of the old WCTU, has worked zealously for eleven years. . . . The National WCTU is now the outstanding prohibition organization of the United States. It is almost wholly responsible for the introduction in Congress of the Sheppard bill proposing dry zones in and around all army camps, and the Bryson bill for national prohibition during the duration of the war. Equally, it is largely responsible for the flood of petitions to Congress for the enactment of this and other prohibition legislation. The national, state and local unions have likewise been active in all local option legislative movements and elections." [34]

YOUTH TEMPERANCE EDUCATION WEEK
· · · · · · · · · ·
BY THE PRESIDENT OF THE UNITED STATES OF AMERICA

A PROCLAMATION

The future of this nation, and perhaps of the world, rests on the integrity and commitment of young Americans who make up almost half of our population. If we neglect the formation of their character, we betray a human trust that transcends the interest of any individual.

Out of a false sophistication, some find it embarrassing to speak of the simple virtues of character that are the mainstays of any great nation or civilization — of duty, sacrifice, fidelity, of sound minds in healthy bodies, of a sense of human brotherhood, love of country, sanctity of the home, purity of ideals.

Yet on these virtues the peace, prosperity, and quality of our society depend.

The condition of our nation today is historically unique. Never has any society come so close to defeating the ancient enemies of poverty, ignorance and ill health. Our social problems loom large in our consciousness, but in the perspective of history, ours is an unprecedented affluence — both in its extent and in its distribution.

And that affluence represents both opportunity and temptation. If it lulls us into complacency, if it dims our moral perception, if it tranquilizes our concern for the suffering of the less fortunate, if it encourages self-indulgence and moral indolence, then it is no blessing but a curse.

NOW, THEREFORE, I, LYNDON B. JOHNSON, President of the United States of America, do hereby proclaim the week beginning April 23, 1967 as Youth Temperance Education Week; and I invite the Governors of the States, the Commonwealth of Puerto Rico, and officials of other areas subject to the jurisdiction of the United States to issue similar proclamations.

IN WITNESS WHEREOF, I have hereunto set my hand and caused the Seal of the United States of America to be affixed.

DONE at the City of Washington this 2 9th day of March, in the year of our Lord nineteen hundred and sixty-seven, and of the Independence of the United States of America the one hundred and ninety-first.

By the President:

Secretary of State

YTC Temperance Education Week Proclaimed by President Lyndon Johnson

Miss Elizabeth Smart, member of the New York State Bar, and editor-owner of an upstate New York weekly newspaper, came to Washington to take charge of the Legislative Bureau in 1940, and served brilliantly in that capacity for almost twenty years through the decades when Mrs. D. Leigh Colvin of New York and Mrs. Glenn G. Hays of Kansas were the national WCTU executives. Upon her death in the fall of 1959, Mrs. Hays, then retiring as National President, filled the Washington office until a more permanent representative could be engaged. By mid-1962, Mrs. Mildred B. Harman, former editor of *Pen-women* and a resident of the Washington area, took charge of the office and continued as Legislative Representative until 1973 when Mrs. Marian B.S. Crymes was appointed.

The power of propaganda as the glamor of television reaches into every home with its subtle implications and sly omissions or embellishments is even more deadly in the 1970's than it was fifty years ago, and used as cleverly by the unprincipled and self-seeking as it was by the Association Against the Prohibition Amendment.

But greater opportunities for scientific research and unparalleled channels of communication have turned scientific theory into scientific fact. Substantial facts about the effect of cigarets on the human body are so impressive that those who gain from their manufacture and sale are obviously worried.

Records showing the extreme cost in money and lives in alcohol-related traffic accidents and in crime are becoming so voluminous that it seems probable they will demand reaction. Looking into the future it seems certain that the time will come when once again citizens of a perceptive country will rise against the all pervasive evil of beverage alcohol.

The more recent years have not been idle ones for the Bureau of Legislation. Numerous bills relating to child welfare, drugs, international relations, cigarets, the sale of beer and liquor have been adequately opposed or supported. Highly publicized confrontation with liquor lobbyists in repeated hearings on alcoholic beverage advertising and airline liquor will be reported in a later chapter.

The WCTU's Bureau of Legislation is well known to Congressional Committee chairmen and to a number of government agencies. Its help is sought by other organizations as well as by individuals when legislation which concerns the welfare of mankind is at stake.

Chapter 5

EDUCATION FOR ABSTINENCE

Even though Scientific Temperance Instruction had been a significant and wisely administered department of the WCTU work since 1880, education for abstinence and on the effects of beverage alcohol did not become a major activity of the organization until more than fifty years later. Work with children and youth and in the schools had flourished but the overriding emphasis had been on efforts to outlaw saloons, to abolish the liquor traffic.

When the Eighteenth Amendment was repealed, after thirteen years of national prohibition, the WCTU leaders recognized that they must gird themselves to cope with an adversary even more powerful than that which the Crusaders of 1873 had faced. The distillers and brewers would leave no stone unturned to recoup the fortunes they had lost in the dry years. Now they had the advantage of being licensed by the government, their product taxed so that nation, state and city received revenue from every drink sold.

Taking her cue from an advertisement which appeared in November 19, 1932, *Brewing Industry* magazine, Mrs. Ida B. Wise Smith, National WCTU President, launched a program of PREVENTION, in capital letters, to be implemented largely through alcohol education and projects for children and youth.

One paragraph in the challenging article, prepared by an advertising agency for the brewers' trade magazine, stood out, "Not one-tenth of one per cent of the youth in college know what really good American beer tastes like. To them it is little more than a name. They will have to be educated." [1]

Education for abstinence had always been basic to the WCTU philosophy. Few of the young people growing up under the protection of prohibition had learned to drink. Obviously, heroic efforts on the part of the liquor interests would attempt to change that situation.

Another paragraph in the *Brewing Industry* article defined their objective, "But beer can be restored to its former favor in colleges, which means the youth of the land. It cannot be done overnight." [2]

The WCTU recognized an urgent need to teach both youth and adults what alcohol is and what it does. The new director of Scientific Temperance Instruction, Miss Bertha Rachel Palmer, former Superintendent of Public Instruction in North Dakota, undertook the assignment. After a year of intensive study at the Bureau of Scientific Temperance Federation library in Boston, Miss Palmer outlined three immediate needs—a training program for teachers, scientifically factual educational materials on alcohol and other narcotics, alcohol education as a part of regular school instruction.

She prepared for teacher use, "A Syllabus on Alcohol Education." Approximately 140,000 copies were printed and circulated during the next fifteen years. Her booklet, "What Alcohol Is and What It Does," was a short course in alcohol education for lay leaders. Simple, easily performed experiments revealed that the qualities of alcohol as a dehydrant and solvent, which make it so valuable to industry, outside the body, are the very qualities which make it harmful inside the body, as a beverage.

Many of the earlier textbooks in physiology and hygiene had presented alcohol as a stimulant. More advanced research had shown that alcohol is a narcotic depressant, not a stimulant, and that its earliest and most ready effect is upon the central nervous system, upon the brain centers which enable human beings to have judgment, reasoning power, self-control. That was the fact which Miss Palmer insisted must be emphasized. In the mechanized world of the 20th century, any beverage which had a tendency to slow and dull the ability to judge, was far more dangerous than it had been in horse and buggy days.

That emphasis has prevailed in the hundreds of thousands of printed materials and visual aids which the WCTU has originated or sponsored in the last forty years as well as in the teacher training seminars.

Alcohol education training courses for teachers were conducted by Miss Palmer each year from 1936 through 1944. Her students spent the months

DIRECTORS OF SCIENTIFIC TEMPERANCE INSTRUCTION

Mrs. Mary H. Hunt
1879-1906

Mrs. Elizabeth G.
Middleton
1918-1922

Mrs. Edith Smith Davis
1907-1918

Bertha Rachel Palmer
1933-1944

Estelle Bozeman
1944-1959

Cora Frances Stoddard
1922-1933

70

NARCOTIC EDUCATION CONSULTANT

Miss Helen M. Allen
1959-

A Narcotic Education booth at the
National Education Association Convention, Atlantic City, New Jersey

of January, February and March in Evanston, where the WCTU had assembled a library of several thousand volumes on alcohol and related problems. Upon completing Miss Palmer's course, many students were qualified to teach similar courses in teacher training colleges. In 1942, summer courses in alcohol education were offered in fifteen colleges in nine states.[3]

Miss Estelle Bozeman of Georgia, a student under Miss Palmer, became Director of Alcohol Education for the National WCTU when Miss Palmer retired in 1944. Meeting the demand for a summer course which could be attended by teachers in service, Miss Bozeman enlisted the cooperation of Northwestern University. A plan was set up which enabled students coming to Evanston for the Narcotics Education course to enroll in designated credit courses at Northwestern. Throughout the six-week summer session at the University, students who had chosen special assignments in narcotics spent from two to six hours a day in the WCTU classroom and library.

Miss Helen M. Allen, an Ohio high school teacher, who became Consultant for the WCTU Narcotic Education Bureau upon the retirement of Miss Bozeman in 1960, reported in 1966 that the summer course in health education at Northwestern had been changed to a three-week workshop. Sixteen teachers earned WCTU certificates in 1966 as well as their credits at Northwestern.

Throughout these years, a well-attended ten-day summer course has been taught in August at Chautauqua, N. Y. State WCTU organizations have aided materially by interesting qualified teachers in these courses and by awarding scholarships sufficient to meet a large portion of the expense required to attend a session.

Directors of education for the WCTU have consistently emphasized the importance of acquainting school administrators and teachers with the program and materials of the WCTU. Conferences with the heads of the departments of education of the various states and exhibits at nationwide educational conventions have received major attention. In 1969, exhibits were maintained at the national conventions of the American Association of School Administrators, American Association of Physical Education, Health and Recreation, National Secondary School Principals, National Department of Elementary School Principals, National Education Association, National Sunday School Association and Central State Association of Independent Schools.

Hundreds of classroom teachers and school administrators register each year at these exhibits requesting sample materials for alcohol education in the school room. Miss Allen reported in 1969 that filling these requests required a mailing list of almost 6000 addresses.

On a par with the educational work in cooperation with the public schools have been the WCTU projects specifically designed for children and youth. In each of these fields a full time director with offices and secretarial help in Evanston has been continuously employed since 1922.

Loyal Temperance Legion

The ingenuity and originality of Miss Anna Adams Gordon, who launched the children's work in her early years as secretary to Frances Willard, in writing stirring songs and playlets and in originating challenging projects and materials, have been matched, even surpassed, by the long line of talented women who have, through the years, administered the Loyal Temperance Legion, children's branch of the WCTU.

Miss Mary B. Ervin of Ohio was Loyal Temperance Legion Secretary in 1922 when a spacious office was provided for the use of that branch in the new Headquarters Building in Evanston. She was succeeded by Mrs. Flora Kay Hanson of Illinois, who served from 1928 to 1932. Miss Lenadell Wiggins of Pennsylvania took charge from 1933 to 1949, when Mrs. S. J. Houlle of Illinois became Secretary. Upon Mrs. Houlle's resignation in 1954, Miss Jean Hansen of South Dakota was appointed and served until after her marriage in 1965. Miss Shirley Hasselquist of Nebraska assumed the office at that time and continued to serve through 1972.

The half century of Loyal Temperance Legion under these qualified leaders has been marked by numerous innovative and constructive activities. Always governed by a basic emphasis on total abstinence and good citizenship, a wide variety of study, work and humanitarian projects have kept hundreds of thousands of youngsters busy "Having Fun While We Learn." Each national leader has paid tribute to the untiring perseverance of community leaders upon whom work with children depends. Millions more children would enjoy LTL if local leaders could be found to supervise them.

Following World War I, LTL members adopted French orphans and

Anna Adams Gordon
National President 1914-1925

earned or collected the money to support them. In the 1940's, during a three month campaign, they raised $2000, enough to purchase forty milk goats for undernourished children in war-devastated Japan. Their contribution abetted the efforts of a Commission on World Service of the Evangelical and Reformed Church.

Constance Houlle's mitten project brought floods of warm handknit mittens which were forwarded to children all over the world. Garden seeds were sent to the Phillipines. In the 1950's special arrangements were made to provide books for children in areas where books were unavailable. In 1958, $1400 was contributed for school kits for refugees from communist China in Hong Kong. 70,000 children needed these kits costing $1 each.

Miss Hansen continued the "Shoes Across the Sea" project into the early 1960's. Thousands of dollars, channeled through CARE, bought $5 packages containing six pairs of sneaker-type shoes for Korean orphans two to twelve years of age. In 1968, Miss Hasselquist reported that sufficient money had been sent to Botswana, South Africa, to pay for powdered milk and cooking oil for 460 children.

Missionary giving has been matched by service projects at home. Local LTL's have installed drinking fountains and park benches in children's playgrounds, planted trees in parks and flowers on church lawns, initiated clean-up campaigns. One group placed temperance safety posters in gas stations at Christmas time. Many have adopted senior citizens or handicapped persons, caring for their yards and running their errands. Hundreds have entered floats in parades and prepared exhibits in cooperation with community events.

Yearly reports give only slight indication of the ingenuity and originality which have resulted in an infinite variety of attractively designed study materials and promotional activities for the LTL. Themes such as "Skyways to Abstinence" and "Junior Citizens on Parade" have found eager acceptance. Playlets, mobiles, puppets and filmstrips have been as widely used in the LTL as in any kindergarten. Coloring sheets based on nursery rhymes with cleverly adapted "abstinence" verses were originated in 1954 and printed by the 100,000's. Still popular, 30,000 were sold in 1969. Speaking contests and picnics appeal to the children of the 20th century as they did to those of the nineteenth. LTL Day camps, instituted in 1959, have become increasingly popular in this motorized recreation-conscious era. 185 were held in 1969.

A jingle written by Vicki Olsen, faithful and talented office secretary, describes well the breadth and vitality of the Loyal Temperance Legion:

We belong to the LTL. That's Loyal Temperance Legion!

Our members live in various lands, with groups in many a region.

While having fun we also learn, and learn we surely do.

The way of abstinence is ours; for that we know is true!

The liquor ads have no appeal, despite what they allege.

We know they're false and furthermore, we're governed by our pledge.

To principle we must adhere. We grow in grace each day.

We're guided into doing right. We follow Jesus' way.

We learn to be good citizens—to do the things we should.

We're banded by world friendship ties into one brotherhood.

When we work and when we play, we strive to do things well;

For we are proud and happy to belong to LTL!

Youth Temperance Council

Equally difficult to chronicle in a few hundred words is the youth work of the WCTU. As an organized group, it came into being as the Young Women's Branch in 1893 with Mrs. Frances J. Barnes of New York as general secretary. The active participation of thousands of young men as honorary members caused the name of the auxiliary to be changed to Young People's Branch in 1909. The distinctive and extensive youth-oriented program, based on the principles which undergird all WCTU activity, dictated a decision in 1934 to adopt the name of Youth Temperance Council. That title continues to label appropriately the hundreds of attractive, dedicated young people who so wholeheartedly pursue "A Good Time with a Purpose."

The young people have their carefully outlined study programs, continuing emphasis on Christian principles and character building activities throughout the year. But summer camps are the highlight of the YTC year in most states. Free from school, YTC members, with their sponsors and instructors, concentrate on worship, study, planning and fun oftentimes under the leadership of the National YTC Secretary. Miss Ethel Riddle of West Virginia, YTC Secretary, 1952 to 1959, drove slightly over 25,000 miles during her first fifteen months in the office.[4] Miss Sarah Ward of Indiana in her five years as secretary, 1964-1969, drove approximately 100,000 miles attending camps and conventions in 38 states.[5] Miss Ward

76

*Loyal Temperance Legion
World's WCTU Convention, 1971*

*Governor Tawes, Maryland, hands Youth Temperance Education Week,
1960, Proclamation to Maryland YTC President, John Ways*

asserted, "The camp program is our most important tool." [6]

Youth Temperance Education Week was a project which brought wide and favorable publicity to the temperance movement in the 1950's. Organized as a state project in Virginia and West Virginia in the 1940's, it was adopted as a National YTC project in 1954.

During a selected week in April, young people in various states projected alcohol education films for school, church and civic organizations, spoke and led discussions, displayed exhibits, conducted and participated in radio and television interviews. Ministers cooperated by preaching temperance sermons and by inviting YTC members to make brief statements from their pulpits.

The growing popularity of YTE week as a project was evidenced by the number of state governors who issued official proclamations designating specific dates for statewide observance. In 1954, YTE week was officially proclaimed in twelve states. By 1958, proclamations were signed by 38 governors and the American Temperance Society printed a feature story about the project in its popular youth magazine, LISTEN.

The annual report of youth work for 1959, read, "Governors of 45 states (including the Commissioner of the District of Columbia and the Governor of Puerto Rico) issued Proclamations for Youth Temperance Education Week, April 12-19, 1959." [7]

By 1965, plans were underway to secure a Presidential Proclamation for YTE Week. Through the cooperation of Senator Everett M. Dirksen and Congressman Donald Rumsfeld, both of Illinois, resolutions were introduced in the Federal Congress authorizing such a proclamation. Pursuing the tortuous way of all Federal legislation through committee, Senate, House, conference, the Resolution was adopted in time for President Lyndon B. Johnson to issue a precedent-breaking proclamation for the nation-wide observance of the fourth week in April, 1967. A copy of that unique document appears here.

Nation-wide projects of popular appeal have challenged abstaining youth throughout the years as they have been motivated by Winona R. Jewell, Colorado, 1928-1932; Helen Louise Byrnes, Iowa, 1933-1938; Martha Smyth Cooper, Ohio, 1939-1943; Regina Moede, Washington, 1944-1948; Erlaine Weaver, Ohio, 1949-1951; Ethel Riddle, West Virginia, 1952-1959; Irene

Curtis, Alabama, 1960-1963; Sarah F. Ward, Indiana, 1964-1969; Rosalita J. Leonard, Pennsylvania, 1970-.

In 1928 more than 350,000 young people affixed their signatures to "A Patriotic Roll Call," pledging "allegiance to the Flag of the United States of America . . . determination to abstain from all intoxicating liquors . . . to enroll for law observance." In 1931, as the campaign for repeal of National Prohibition plagued America, 1,045,872 youth pledged "total abstinence and law observance" in a Youth's Roll Call, which, carried by 165 young people, was presented to President Herbert Hoover at the White House.[8]

Aware of the cold beer consistently made available to boys in military service, the National Youth Temperance Council sponsored a drive to send Pepsi Cola to USO Clubs throughout Viet Nam. $13,000 was raised and donated for this purpose in 1968.

"My Action Commitment" prepared by Martha Smyth Cooper states simply the ideals and motives which govern the Youth Temperance Council—

"Being convinced that the use of alcoholic beverages
　　　Hinders me as a Christian,
　　　Interferes with life at its best,
　　　Cripples our nation's strength,
　　I, therefore, commit myself not only to personal abstinence
from alcoholic beverages but to a program of action against
alcohol in my community." [9]

Narcotic Education, the Youth Temperance Council and the Loyal Temperance Legion are the chief channels of an organization which devotes 95% of its time, effort and money to education. Many other educational emphases are pursued with persistence and imagination.

Other Educational Channels

Always dependent upon and appreciative of the church, upon Christian citizens, the National WCTU early sought to provide for regular temperance teaching in the Sunday School. Working through the International Sunday School Association, WCTU leaders appealed for a regular Bible study lesson emphasizing the values of abstinence. In 1887 the International Sunday School Lesson Committee began preparing Quarterly Temperance Lessons for their Uniform Series Bible Study Course.[10] Ten years later

Theobald Faces The Facts
Popular Animated Cartoon Film Produced in 1959

Willard Memorial Library
dedicated in 1940

a "World's Temperance Sunday," suggested by the Sunday School Union of London, was adopted with the suggestion that the fourth quarterly temperance lesson be combined with this universal date.

A committee, which now prepares the Uniform lessons, appointed by the Division of Christian Education of the National Council of Churches stated in 1951, "The committee on the Uniform Series believes in temperance education and is concerned that provision be made for this in the most effective way. Its procedure in the outlines is to designate one lesson each quarter for special temperance emphasis . . . related as fully as possible to the Bible material from which the lessons are developed." [11] In August 1971, three Bible School lessons were devoted to the social results of beverage alcohol.[12]

Appropriate material based upon the International outline is prepared regularly for all age groups by WCTU specialists. These printed lesson helps and supplementary materials such as filmstrips, Vacation Bible School kits, flannelgraphs, posters have appeared frequently on the "recommended" list in various denominational publications and are widely used.

Speech, poster and essay contests have been used repeatedly as educational devices by the National WCTU. Writing and poster contests have taken many forms and appealed to a wide variety of age groups.

Speech contests, first adopted as a 'department of work' by the National WCTU in 1887, became enormously popular in the first decades of the 20th century when Community Chautauquas and Summer Assemblies were the rage. It was not unusual for a half dozen young orators to memorize temperance readings and compete for award medals as a featured program of the scheduled summer chautauqua.[13]

The medals provided for awards by the Honorable W. Jennings Demorest, temperance advocate of New York, set the pattern for the competition. The winner of a silver medal was eligible to compete for a gold medal and go on up in the increasingly stiff competition to participate in pearl, diamond and grand diamond contests. Mr. Demorest recognized the public speaking contests as a remarkably efficient educational device which gave training to the speakers while it imparted information to their audiences.

The permanency of the speech contest as a WCTU project was more or less assured when a $5000 bequest was left to the organization in 1928 in memory of Ada Mohn Landis.[14] The income from this fund furnishes cash awards for an annual contest in which writers prepare manuscripts suitable for speech contests. Awards went to authors in California, Nebraska, Indiana, Colorado, Massachusetts and Queensland, Australia, in 1954.

Fifteen hundred speaking contests were reported in 40 different states in 1959 in spite of television. A grand diamond contest is a feature of the National Convention program each year. The winner at Los Angeles in 1970 was Rhonda Lee Carter of Middletown, Ohio.

In the early 1970's as the television networks gave inordinate attention and exposure to recalcitrant, confused and unprincipled youth, it was refreshing and reassuring to mingle with the 500 young people who came to Chicago to attend the World's WCTU Convention. Carrying the Torch of Total Abstinence, youth delegates from twenty-five states and seven foreign countries, led by YTC Secretary, Rosalita Leonard, packed the stage of the convention hall to exemplify the wholesome and realistic Christian principles which have been the basis and emphasis of the WCTU for one hundred years.

Chapter 6

TO LET THE PEOPLE KNOW

Typically the women who have been leaders in the Woman's Christian Temperance Union have been platform women. Annie T. Wittenmyer, first National president, had spoken in every state in the Union inaugurating Home Missionary Society plans for the Methodist Church before the WCTU was organized.[1] As WCTU president "she labored tirelessly in the lecture field speaking sometimes six evenings in the week." In 1875 she attended forty-six large conventions.[2]

Frances Willard's "silver tongue" contributed enormously to her lasting fame. The language of an 1875 newspaper report of a Willard lecture would seem extreme had it not been repeated so consistently, "The least that can be said about her address is that it was finished in style, perfect in oratory, logical in argument, and irresistible in appeal." [3]

The white marble statue of Frances Willard in Statuary Hall of the nation's Capitol depicts her in characteristic pose, standing at a speaker's podium, manuscript in hand. In 1883 she had visited every state and territory in the United States, speaking in the capital cities of all except Arizona and Idaho.[4]

Speakers were in demand during the first forty years of WCTU history. Hire a hall, announce a speaker, and the people came. WCTU leaders such as Mary Harris Armor of Georgia and Lillian M. N. Stevens of Maine drew crowds just as effectively as did William Jennings Bryan of Nebraska and Albert J. Beveridge of Indiana.

During its first sixty years the speaker's rostrum and the printed page were the communication media of the WCTU. The women who spoke also wrote. As the motion picture screen, radio and television became

83

established channels of communication, the WCTU took advantage of their availability and efficiency.

Within six months after the organizing convention of the WCTU in the fall of 1874, an official publication, *The Woman's Temperance Union,* had been inaugurated. The national president, Mrs. Annie T. Wittenmyer, had a publication of her own, *Christian Woman.* Her publishing experience helped.[5] Three years later, the name of the monthly magazine was changed to *Our Union.* The 1882 convention voted to consolidate *Our Union* with the *Signal,* a temperance magazine owned by the Woman's Temperance Publishing Association of Chicago. The first issue of *The Union Signal* appeared January 4, 1883.[6]

For the next twenty years the official organ of the National WCTU was financed and published by a non-affiliated association. The Woman's Temperance Publishing Association also published huge quantities of leaflets and pamphlets for the WCTU. They began publishing *The Young Crusader,* a WCTU magazine for children, in 1886.[7]

Manufactures of a wide variety of products advertised extensively in the early day *Union Signal.* Many columns of advertising sought to sell Larkin Soap but Ivory Soap outdid them with beautiful full-page ads in color.

Advertising of health products was continuous. Beecham' pills, grape nuts, Cascarets, condensed milk and remedies for every ailment including bladder trouble, cancer and fits were recommended. Royal Baking Powder advised, "Take care to have your biscuit made with Royal if you would avoid indigestion." [8]

Sears Roebuck was a consistent advertiser. The Wing Piano, Concert and Grand Upright, was pictured beside steam bath cabinets and Emaline Stove Polish. Advertising for drinking fountains probably appeared most often but encyclopedias and hair switches were close seconds.

The Publishing Association was purchased outright by the WCTU in 1903. All periodicals and printed materials have been edited and published since that year at National WCTU Headquarters in Evanston.[9] In 1910 a substantial Literature Building was erected to house the publishing activities. It was dedicated, debt free, on December 6, 1910.[10]

A series of competent and dedicated editors, publishers, and circulation managers have changed formats and printing schedules many times, always

The Young Crusader, Volume One, Number One
January, 1887

with the intent of making WCTU magazines more attractive and readable. Through one hundred years a major problem has been to induce members to subscribe to and read *The Union Signal*. The plea of Lillian M. N. Stevens in 1905, "I must insist that it is not too much to expect that each local union should maintain a subscription list equal to one-fourth its membership," [11] was still appropriate in 1974.

Since April, 1954, color has been effectively used in the *Union Signal* format. The liquor press, as well as WCTU members, noted its improved appearance. A statement by Thomas J. Donovan, executive director of Licensed Beverage Industries, Inc., appeared in November 19, 1954, *Journal of Commerce*. It read in part, "On a nationwide scale, the drys have stepped up their public relations efforts, spruced up their publications, abandoned some of the old propaganda lines and formulated new ones that are apparently designed to appeal to new and younger audiences." [12]

A concrete example of this effort is revealed in a project endorsed by the state WCTU presidents in the fall of 1953. Working with School and College Service of Columbus, Ohio, the National WCTU underwrote the printing of hundreds of thousands of copies of a brightly colored, 32-page booklet, *Alcohol at the Wheel*.

Filled with bluntly stated scientific fact on drinking and driving, generally approved by high school principals and driver education instructors, the booklet filled a recognized need. Service clubs, such as Kiwanis and Rotary, joined local WCTU's and church organizations in purchasing gift copies for high school seniors. In numerous high schools, *Alcohol at the Wheel* was adopted as a text for driver education classes. 250,000 copies were sold the first year.

After twenty years, *Alcohol at the Wheel* is still in demand, a part of the WCTU's effort to let the people know the tragic contribution which beverage alcohol makes to traffic fatalities each year.

The National WCTU Publishing House has always been a big business. One school system in Florida ordered 11,000 copies of "Dope on Drug Abuse" by Robert Seliger, M.D. in 1970. 53,500 copies of "Double Danger-Drugs and Alcohol" were sold in 19 months in 1972. The National WCTU Publishing House sold more than $6000 worth of materials at the 1971 World's WCTU Convention in Chicago.

Visual Aids

Visual aids, films and filmstrips, produced by the National WCTU have been widely used and highly recommended. "The Beneficent Reprobate," a three-reel 35 mm. black and white sound film, would be considered too lengthy and too drab for today's school room. It was produced for the National WCTU in 1934, the first motion picture to emphasize the beneficial effects of alcohol outside the body as compared with the harmful effects of alcohol inside the body. Prints of the film sold for $75.00. Seventy-five prints of the film were deposited with the YMCA Motion Picture Department for loan throughout the country. Within one year all prints were booked for months in advance.[13]

So factual was its content, so basic its logic, that prints continued to sell long after more modern productions were available. The U.S. Army Signal Corps Pictorial Center purchased twelve prints of "Beneficent Reprobate" in 1954.[14]

During the intervening twenty years, ten more motion pictures on 16 mm. film, some in color, and eight filmstrips had been produced. Most of them were graded for school use. "It's the Brain That Counts" became so popular that it was incorporated into a new "The Brain Is the Reason" when old model automobiles in the original demanded a new format.

The Visual Instruction Bureaus of many state universities approved and became depositories for WCTU films. The larger city school systems owned their own prints. Los Angeles schools reported showing "Liquid Lore" 1029 times to 97,995 pupils in 1957.[15] The Navy Chaplains' Film Program and the International Bureau Against Alcoholism, Lausanne, Switzerland, were among those who purchased prints of "It's the Brain That Counts."[16]

The National WCTU continues to lead in the production of films concerning beverage alcohol. "Theobald Faces the Facts," an animated cartoon, was chosen to participate in the American Film Festival in New York in April, 1960.[17] "Behind the Skyscrapers," a documentary, was among twenty-seven finalists at the San Francisco International Film Festival in 1962.[18] It was in competition with 250 films from fifteen countries.

Communities, large and small, continue to take advantage of a teaching device not available when the WCTU originated its crusade for abstinence. 1970 reports revealed that New Hampshire teachers had signed up for the

RECORDING SECRETARIES, 1874-1949

Mrs. Mary C. Johnson
1874-1878

Mrs. Mary Woodbridge
1878-1893

Mrs. Nelle G. Burger
1934-1944

Mrs. Clara C. Hoffman
1894-1906

Mrs. Glenn G. Hays
1944-1950

Mrs. Elizabeth Preston
Anderson
1906-1926

Mrs. Sara H. Hoge
1926-1934

RECORDING SECRETARIES

1950-1973

Mrs. Fred J. Tooze
1950-1956

Mrs. T. Roy Jarrett
1956-1959

Mrs. J. Kenneth W. Miller
1959-

use of WCTU films in twenty-five schools; Mississippi youth in thirty-nine schools and churches had seen "The Choice Is Yours"; 124 films which Michigan WCTU has deposited in two film libraries were shown in 1970 to 54,355 viewers; 19,000 persons had viewed WCTU films placed in Nebraska State Health Department Library.

Mayor Samuel Yorty of Los Angeles presented a Commendatory Scroll to the City Federation of WCTU for its contribution of educational films as a part of the effort to minimize juvenile delinquency.[19] Incomplete reports indicate that forty or fifty thousand Los Angeles school children view WCTU films each year.

In 1968 National WCTU furnished a copy of "The Brain Is the Reason" to Kyushu Christian Mission in Japan for translation into the Japanese language. Mrs. Masako Munakata of Japan reported in 1971 that the film was the first on alcohol to be presented in the Japanese language and was widely used. In response to popular demand, the National WCTU produced a number of filmstrips on addictive drugs in 1970. "Drugs— Kicks or Killers" was cited for excellence by the 1971 International Film and TV Festival in New York and won first place in the filmstrip section of the National Visual Communications Association.[20]

New Opportunities

Radio and television offered new opportunities to the WCTU to present scientific facts about alcohol and to publicize objectives and program. Local radio stations have been generous with public service time. Nationally produced transcriptions have been regularly used in many states. National officers and other speakers have invariably been invited to use radio time in communities visited.

Before television, the radio networks were consistent in contributing time to National WCTU Conventions. On June 30, 1933, a part of President Boole's address on "Prohibition at the Crossroads" was heard on a nationwide radio broadcast. She was speaking at the 59th National Convention in Milwaukee. Enroute to Tulsa, Oklahoma, for a WCTU Convention in 1936, Mrs. Ida B. Wise Smith stopped in St. Louis to speak for fifteen minutes on a nationwide CBS radio broadcast. Each of the three nationwide chains, CBS, Mutual and NBC, gave fifteen minutes of national network time to the 1939 convention which convened in Rochester, N. Y. Daily broadcasts were made over local stations.[21]

Local leaders have been resourceful and well received in their use of public service time on local radio. On New Years' Eve, 1955, a popular Anchorage, Alaska, station repeated Mrs. Blanch Pennington's natural fruit beverage recipes in the interest of highway safety.[22] The National WCTU continued to furnish radio releases for local use in 1968.[23]

Public Relations Counsel

Since 1945, the National WCTU has retained the services of the Harry E. Caylor Public Relations Organization. The prudent and efficient service of the Caylors has resulted in continuing and wide publicity concerning the progress of the WCTU and the claims of the liquor interests. In 1949, Mr. Caylor wrote "The Black Book of Repeal." Factual and concise, it has been updated at intervals and continues to be an informative source.

Much of the nationwide magazine and television coverage of WCTU personalities and activities has originated in Caylor news releases. National Conventions, attended by women from every corner of the United States, have always made news. A partial survey of newspaper stories concerning the 1958 convention in Washington, D. C. measured 6800 column inches in forty-seven states.[24] Los Angeles television stations gave extensive coverage to the 1970 convention with Mrs. Tooze, Mrs. Jarrett, and other officers appearing for interviews on twenty different occasions.[25] Eight publications, including *The New York Times,* sent reporters to Chicago to cover the 1971 World's WCTU Convention. The metropolitan Chicago dailies printed 680 column inches on the week-long event.[26]

Books

The National WCTU has sold thousands of books. A few have been printed by the organization itself. The first of these was a 700-page story of her life written by Frances E. Willard and published in 1889. "Glimpses of Fifty Years," the Willard autobiography, was commissioned by action of the delegates at the 1887 National Convention. Undertaking the prodigious task, Miss Willard moved into a downtown Chicago hotel where she spent three months in virtual seclusion, writing 1200 pages by hand with pen and ink.[27] 36,000 copies of the autobiography were sold six months after its publication.[28]

Less than ten years later, "The Beautiful Life of Frances E. Willard" appeared. This memorial volume, written by Anna A. Gordon, contained numerous tributes from well-known leaders in the temperance cause and similarly sincere expressions from notables such as Booker T. Washington, Margaret E. Sangster and the Rev. Edward Everett Hale.[29]

Elizabeth Putnam Gordon was asked to write a history of the first fifty years of the Woman's Christian Temperance Union. Her "Women Torch-bearers" was published in 1924, soon after National Prohibition became the law of the land. She was able to present a story of half a century of growth and accomplishment. Mentioning the small beginning in 1874, she wrote, "Today it is a mighty host with a membership of half a million and a large following of cooperating, home-loving women." [30]

"Give Prohibition Its Chance," written by Dr. Ella A. Boole in 1929 and copyrighted by Fleming H. Revell Company, was an effort to place before the public the true facts about the economic advantages of National Prohibition.[31]

In 1949, a history of the Woman's Christian Temperance Union's seventy-five years was published. Mrs. Helen E. Tyler, newspaperwoman and former editor of the *Union Signal,* wrote "Where Prayer and Purpose Meet." [32] Thoroughly documented and professionally produced her 300-page WCTU story is basic to any serious study of the temperance movement. 8000 copies have been sold.

The most recent book published by the National WCTU, "The Christian Case for Abstinence," was a by-product of the organization's Eightieth Anniversary observance. Among the anniversary projects, suggested by President Hays, was a Temperance Sermon Contest. Ministers were requested to send copies of temperance sermons which they had preached to regular Sunday morning congregations in 1954. Distinguished judges were secured. Cash awards were offered. Manuscripts were received from thirty-nine states.[33]

So excellent were the sermons that Association Press of New York City suggested a compilation of the prize-winners in book form. "The Christian Case for Abstinence," a 200-page book, was published in October, 1955. Selected by the Evangelical Book Club for its October Book of the Month,[34] 7000 copies went to its subscribers. A total of 13,000 copies were printed and sold.[35]

The WCTU has contributed extensively to the distribution of outstand-

Highway Poster at 1955 Convention, Long Beach

ing books from other publishers. It has stocked and sold 9000 copies of Upton Sinclair's "Cup of Fury." So factual and authoritative is the information in "The Amazing Story of Repeal" by Fletcher Dobyns that the WCTU has refused to allow it to go out of print. Copyrighted in 1940, "The Amazing Story" is timeless in content. That it may continue to be available for research, the WCTU arranged for its reprint in 1965.

Frances E. Willard Memorial Library for Alcohol Research, constructed at the National Headquarters in Evanston and dedicated in 1940, has filled a need and attracted the patronage of many serious students. Among its 4000 volumes are out-of-print as well as current treatises on the scientific, economic and social aspects of the alcohol problem. Unsurpassed is the library collection of journals, scrapbooks and other memorabilia relating to the history of the Woman's Christian Temperance Union and the temperance movement in general. Among the rare books still available for study are *Woman and Temperance* by Frances E. Willard, copyrighted by Park Publishing Co., Hartford, Connecticut, in 1883, *Women's War on Whiskey* by J. H. Beadle, published at Cincinnati in 1874, and *History of the Woman's Temperance Crusade* by Annie Wittenmyer, printed in Philadelphia in 1878.

Outdoor Advertising

State and local abstinence organizations have extended their efforts to reach the public by the use of road signs. Missouri WCTU initiated a Safe Driving Campaign in 1937. The WCTU supplied posters for eighty billboards which an outdoor advertising association donated for their use for three months.[36] In 1954, the National WCTU had large billboard posters, 12 feet by 25 feet, lithographed in color in four designs. These were offered to local sponsors at $8 per poster. The response was heartening.[37]

Memphis, Tennessee, unions rented ten billboards.[38] Local unions in Alabama[39] and at North Platte, Nebraska,[40] erected their own. Outdoor advertising companies in both Minnesota and Pennsylvania supplemented the rented billboards by donated space.[39] A poster erected by Syracuse, Kansas, WCTU could be seen by passengers on Santa Fe streamliners as well as by motorists on a nearby transcontinental highway.[41] The WCTU erected signs on all main highways entering Chattanooga.[40]

In less than six months, posters were on display in twenty-one states.[39] The Durban Sunday School Association of South Africa wrote requesting

THE NEW CRUSADE MARCH

Mrs. C. H. M.   Mrs. Claude H. Mayo

1. Do   you hear the tramping of the New Crusade, Try-ing to re-pair the
2. Do   you hear the call-ing of the Youth's Cru-sade, Calling on all mothers.
3. Not by might nor pow-er saith our Great Command But by my Spir-it

wreck Re-peal has made? We will in-crease our number while we're marching on,
to come to their aid? Make the path-way safe they're pleading in de-spair,
you will claim the land. So with Christ as Captain we will nev-er fear,

CHORUS

Till the vic-to-ry is won.
Hear them call-ing ev-'ry-where. From the Hills of Maine to the Ev-er-glades,
For the vic-to-ry is near.

From the Great Old At-lantic to the West-ern Plains, You will hear the march

of the New Cru-sade, 'Till we con-quer the Foe and raise our ban - ner.

95

posters, explaining that the Province of Natal is largely English speaking and their citizens would find the poster messages most pertinent.[42]

At least one of the posters carried its message to a prejudiced audience in an unanticipated manner. A trade journal of the brewing industry printed a clear cut picture of the poster originated by Mr. and Mrs. George L. Ehrman and the Ben Whitacres of Kokomo, Indiana.

Poster No. 1, showing in graphic color a sadly wrecked automobile, carried the slogan, "It was only beer but its companion was death." *Modern Brewery Age* reproduced it as an example of the manner in which the WCTU pinpoints alcohol's contribution to traffic fatalities. Its editor commented that the poster "is typical of the propaganda war waged against beer by the organization." [43]

The WCTU Sings

The Temperance Glee Clubs suggested in the Plan of Work adopted at the first convention in 1874 failed to materialize on any large scale, but music has always held a prominent place in many phases of WCTU activity. Anna A. Gordon's book of "Marching Songs for Young Crusaders" was first published in 1886. 25,000 copies were printed the first year.[44] 100,000 were in sold in three years.[45] Shirley Hasselquist and Sarah Ward cooperated in 1971 to produce the tuneful "We're Going To Be Sensible." Songbooks for young people and adults have been continuously among WCTU publications.

The unique "Victory" solo with its Swiss mountain melody and cornet obligato was the musical peak of each annual convention during prohibition years.[46] But the real music of the WCTU has been in the well-loved and familiar songs played and sung by the members themselves.

"All 'round the world the ribbon white is twined," written by Katherine Lente Stevenson, corresponding Secretary, 1894-1898, continues a favorite.[47] Mrs. Lorena B. Galloway of Bushnell, Illinois, composer of "Back to God, O America," won the WCTU song writing contest in 1946 with "The Battle Hymn of the WCTU." The marching music of her "Pray and Educate; Pray and Legislate; Pray and Agitate till every heart is stirred . . ." thrills those who listen as well as those who sing.[48]

The same lilting quality has made the "New Crusade March," written by Mrs. Claude H. Mayo of Lake Charles, Louisiana, in 1954, a lasting favorite. Its "Do you hear the tramping of the New Crusade, Trying to repair the wreck Repeal has made?" [49] lifts the same timeless challenge as that sounded by the early Crusaders as they sang "Give to the winds thy fears." [50]

Chapter 7

THEY CARE ENOUGH

As hundreds of thousands of fine young Americans fought to save the Vietnamese from Communism in the late 1960's, the National WCTU added its prestige to the effort of the Youth Temperance Council by raising thousands of dollars to buy cold soft drinks to be dispensed by the USO in Vietnam.

Maryland WCTU had pioneered this appealing project in 1967. Their first check for $556.00 had been taken to Saigon by an official of the Pepsi Cola company who had given it to the Chief of Chaplains for the purchase of non-alcoholic beverages for the soldiers. The gift provided for 300 cases of soft drinks.[1]

In 1968, "Pepsi Cola for our Servicemen in Vietnam" was enthusiastically promoted by YTC members throughout the United States. With the help of local WCTU organizations and innumerable civic and church groups, the National YTC raised $10,300 for this purpose in a special three months drive.[2]

In the third year, 1969, the Pepsi drive became a WCTU project for the first time. The Pepsi Cola company arranged for the WCTU to purchase their product at wholesale prices. The National WCTU Treasurer's report at the 1970 convention in Los Angeles revealed $63,000 had been collected for the project in less than three years.[3]

An executive director of USO wrote in May, 1970, "Thousands upon thousands of these men will know that the ladies in your organization *do care!* The WCTU has made it possible for the USO to dispense, free of charge, more than two hundred thousand containers of Pepsi Cola, and that is a magnificent contribution to the troops. A cold Pepsi Cola is a

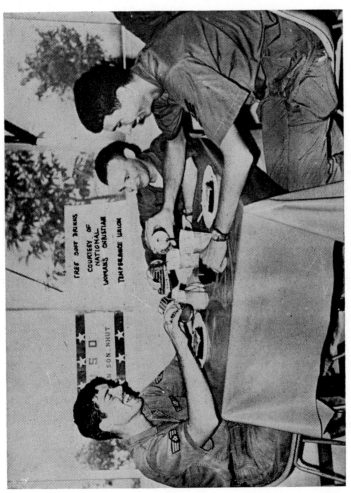

U. S. Service Men Enjoy Soft Drinks in Vietnam
courtesy of Woman's Christian Temperance Union

welcome, refreshing morale builder for our troops," [4]

Humanitarian and philanthropic projects are not new to the WCTU. Records of the years show hundreds of thousands of dollars contributed, innumerable unique and effective devices advanced in the effort to alleviate need and bring comfort.

Regular funds coming into the WCTU Treasury are ear-marked for a continuing program of education, legislation and administration. Money for charitable purposes must come from other sources through the extra effort of dedicated service.

Frances Willard was in England in 1896 when persecution of the Armenians began in Turkey. Hurrying to France she observed the destitution of the Armenian refugees crowding into Marseilles. Working with the Salvation Army, she helped to establish a food and refuge station. In response to her appeal John D. Rockefeller contributed $5000, the National WCTU, $10,000. [5] In addition WCTU members and their friends in the eastern section of the United States opened their homes. Nearly 300 of the exiles came to shelter in America.

This same concern for people of other lands had motivated the WCTU in 1885 when they noted the bewildered aloneness of immigrants entering the United States in enormous numbers. In cooperation with the WCTU of New York, the National WCTU employed a multilingual "missionary" for duty at Ellis Island, New York port of entry for immigrants. [6]

This kindly woman, speaking in several tongues, was often able to aid and reassure the confused aliens. Bent on extending a welcome which could be understood, WCTU members throughout the states fashioned thousands of black sateen bags, equipped them with toilet necessities and sent them to Ellis Island. This WCTU service continued as long as the need existed, about 40 years. [7]

Ellis Island was only one of many missionary activities of the WCTU.

In 1927, the original plan of Laura Gerould Craig of New York was adopted to provide a special fund for "temperance and missions". Local unions making an annual contribution of $5 for this fund were designated as Light Line Unions. In 1927, $10,000 was expended for relief of Mississippi flood victims and more than $3000 for the Near East. [8] Nearly $3000 was paid into the treasury of the World's WCTU.

100

For the next thirty years increasingly large amounts went from the Light Line Unions of the United States to support and expand the work of the World's WCTU, $14,442.50 in 1955, $14,018.75 in 1959.[9]

In recent years a portion of the Light Line funds has been allocated to meet appeals coming from a variety of needs. A letter from the Phillipines asked for WCTU flannelgraphs which had been advertised in *Youth for Christ* magazine. A South African teacher's request for books for 75 high school students training to be teachers was filled. Materials were supplied for the Gila River WCTU on an Indian Reservation in Arizona. One hundred copies of a requested book on alcohol were sent for health classes in a church school for colored students. Brochures and pamphlets translated by Mrs. Clara R. Ports and Mrs. Edith M. Irvine-Rivera were printed in Spanish in quantities sufficient to supply Latin Americans in neighboring countries as well as in the U.S.A.

In 1958 a pastor in Guatemala wrote, "A temperance filmstrip would open the door for me to preach the gospel almost anywhere." [10] National WCTU supplied the filmstrip. Films were sent to supply a need in Greece in 1959, and a projector and filmstrips to the Phillipines.[11] Three films went to a missionary in Burundi, Africa, in 1970. His ability to translate the script into native languages made them usable in many different sections of that huge country.[12]

The States Met Local Needs

In the early days of the organization, state and local unions directed much effort to meeting local needs. In more than one state "schools for wayward girls", established by the WCTU, became state institutions. Kansas WCTU chose Beloit in North Central Kansas as the location for the school they established in 1888. Thirty-three girls were in residence one year later when the state legislature took charge of it as the Kansas Girls' Industrial School. Kansas WCTU had "organized, staffed, housed, equipped, and operated it for thirteen and one-half months." [13] After 85 years this state institution continues at the original location.

Delaware WCTU was responsible for that state's industrial school and provided a large share of its financial support for many years. On the campus of the School, which has moved and expanded several times, are two substantial buildings named for early WCTU leaders. Each local WCTU in Delaware has furnished a room at the School. After 80 years,

Mercy Home for Girls, Manchester, New Hampshire

the local unions continue to make annual gifts of large amounts of fruits and canned goods.[14]

Elizabeth Lund Home in Burlington, Vermont, originated in 1890 when WCTU leaders approached the state legislature with offers of assistance in getting a home for friendless women established. WCTU members, named by the legislature, composed the board charged with getting the project underway. Through the years the WCTU of Vermont has continued its support with gifts of bedding and provisions as well as money.

The Door of Hope mission which an Indianapolis WCTU opend in 1893 for unwed mothers later became a part of the Florence Crittenden Association and is today a part of the Wheeler Mission in Indianapolis.[15] The training school for girls, seven to seventeen, which Michigan WCTU opened in August, 1881, later became the state Industrial Home for Girls. Located at Adrian, Michigan, it consisted of seven cottages occupied by 300 girls in 1899.[16]

New Hampshire owned and operated Mercy Home for Girls for 76 years. The state legislature in 1890 appropriated $5000 for such a facility if the WCTU would raise a like sum and initiate the project. Purchasing a 14-room house at Manchester, the WCTU furnished it and hired a matron. In 1965, New Hampshire WCTU turned the operation over to New England Fellowship of Evangelicals. WCTU leaders continue to serve on the Home's governing board and New Hampshire WCTU provides financial support approximating $9000 per year.[17]

Still functioning as a WCTU project is Benedict Home, Des Moines, Iowa. Opened in 1882 as a home for wayward girls, it operated in that capacity until 1944. A new building was purchased in 1955, designed to accommodate elderly persons, who are its present residents.[18] The Mother Hull Home in Kearney, Nebraska, has been a charge of the WCTU since 1893. Operated at first as a "Hospital", it attained its present status as a home for senior citizens in 1922. Enthusiastically supported as filling a need by the Kearney community, Kearney WCTU conducted a ground breaking ceremony on September 26, 1971, for the purpose of building two additional wings at a cost of $150,000.[19]

Coffee Houses, Reading Rooms

Late in the 19th century, coffee houses and reading rooms were popular

103

Sparta, Wisconsin, Coffee House and Reading Room

projects of local unions. A number of early day reading rooms later became the nucleus for public libraries.

A saloon which had gone out of business was purchased by the Sparta, Wisconsin, WCTU in 1892. Reserving an upper floor for a meeting room, the WCTU opened a coffee house and reading room on the lower floor. Ten cent lunches were made available and business was good.[20]

Hollister, California, WCTU nourished the Reading Room, which they established in 1884, until it "was merged with its 1000 volumes into the beautiful Carnegie Library of the town." [21] Evans Hall, erected by friends of temperance in Evansville, Indiana, in 1878, became the property of Central WCTU in that city and is now the site of the City Library. The WCTU leased the property to the city for 99 years so that a new library building might be erected.[22]

The coffee house, often with Reading Room attached, offered an eating place where no liquor was served. A northern California historian commented, "Everywhere the Coffee House was a refining and reforming factor." [23]

Early issues of the Charleston, South Carolina, *News-Courier* indicated that the first thought of many local unions in that area was to establish a coffee house, "a restaurant of the best character where young men can eat, away from the surroundings of strong drink." [24] The coffee houses in San Jose and Oakland, California, enjoyed a prosperous patronage for more than ten years. Six coffee houses were maintained in San Francisco until the need no longer existed. One did a business of $15,000 a year.[25]

A number of large institutions stand today because of early recognition of a need by the WCTU. Germantown Boys Club in Philadelphia, now a 2000 member club with an impressive Board of Managers, was started in 1887 by the WCTU of Germantown. In that year they equipped a room with books and games and kept it open in the evenings. The Executive Director of the Club wrote in 1958, "From this humble beginning, our club has grown until today we have a large building, outdoor swimming pool, athletic field and summer camp." [26]

Birmingham, Alabama, WCTU founded Mercy Home in 1892. During its first year thirty-nine women and more than forty children were cared for. Some came for only temporary shelter. None were turned away.[27]

From the first, Mercy Home enjoyed the approval and financial support of the citizens and organizations of Birmingham.

Today, Mercy Home, its name changed to Gateway in 1968, occupies a lovely seven acre campus. Nine commodious buildings provide an atmosphere of family living. The Community Chest has assumed a major responsibility for its financing. As in 1892, no child is "turned away." [28]

Another large facility operated for children in need is the Children's Farm Home established and sponsored by Oregon WCTU. Occupying 285 acres of beautiful farm land near Corvallis, Oregon, the Children's Home cares for an average residency of 130 children, ten to eighteen years of age. In addition to the nine cottages in which the children live, the Home has its own elementary school, dispensary, laundry, chapel, commissary, as well as barns and maintenance buildings. The school is operated as a part of the Corvallis City Schools.

The Farm, an ideal environment for growing youngsters, keeps the older ones busy as it teaches them skills. The tons of vegetables, beef and pork produced are consumed at the Home. Financial support comes from the United Fund and state aid to dependent children as well as from the WCTU and approving friends. [29]

Alameda County, California, WCTU established its Frances E. Willard Club in Oakland in 1922, a "home away from home" for working girls receiving salaries of less than $20 per week. They paid less than $20 per month for room and board. When no longer needed for inadequately paid girls, the Club opened its doors to elderly women and continued to function until 1968 when it gave way to urban renewal and Federal housing projects. [30]

Dozens of others could be mentioned. The 13-room building in downtown Washington which the District of Columbia WCTU maintained as a boarding house for employed girls from 1901 to 1946. [31] The Soup Headquarters in Birmingham, Alabama, where WCTU women daily simmered a huge pot of soup and served ten cent lunches to grateful customers in 1915 and 1916. [32] The Carry A. Nation Home in Kansas City, Kansas, where elderly women were cared for by Kansas WCTU for forty years. [33] The rooms maintained as lodging for working women by New Albany, Indiana, WCTU for more than fifty years. Frances Willard Home for Girls in Tulsa, Oklahoma, and WCTU Home for Children, Rockford, Illinois, are others. Allen County, Indiana, operated two residences for "business girls away from home" for a span of thirteen years, until 1962.

A Patriotic Organization

The National WCTU is a patriotic organization. They have supported every war effort of their country, have cooperated without reserve in the conservation of critical supplies. By the same token, they have opposed anything which might cause or encourage war.

The National WCTU president presented a petition with 199,531 personal signatures to Secretary of State Charles Evans Hughes when President Harding called the International Conference for Reduction of Armanents. In 1946, the WCTU opposed peacetime Universal Military Training. WCTU peace effort has consistently emphasized "the principle of cooperation with other nations in matters that will advance the welfare of the people."

Concrete evidence of neighborly cooperation between nations is the International Peace Garden stretching along the Canadian—United States boundary line between North Dakota and Manitoba. Development of acres of parkland along the Canal-to-Canada Highway at this point has continued since 1932. Organizations and individuals, as well as governments, have contributed to make the Garden a permanently beautiful and meaningful spot. In 1955 the National WCTU and Canadian WCTU joined to install two wrought iron garden seats and a drinking fountain of granite in the Peace Panel section of the Formal Garden.[34]

As women of peace, WCTU members have had an overwhelming concern for the men and boys who suffer and sacrifice in military camps and on the battlefield. With ingenuity, resourcefulness and unremitting effort they have reached out a helping hand to lonely, homesick soldier boys in every wartime period in United States history.

Annie Turner Wittenmyer, first president of the National WCTU, was widely known before she assumed that office. In 1862 she had led the women of Iowa in forming a Soldier's Aid Society. Their interest supplied dried fruits for wounded soldiers, and cotton sheets for their beds in the hospital tents. Women in other states followed the Iowa lead, their ministrations bringing a measure of comfort to the wounded of both the Union and Confederate Armies.

Before the close of the war, one hundred diet kitchens had been installed. The Special Diet Kitchen had become a part of the United States Army and Annie T. Wittenmyer was the officer in charge.[35]

Communities and states in which permanent military installations are located have called upon the WCTU for special and continuing services. The San Diego (Calif.) City Federation of WCTU operated the Home Center for Service Men.

A California historian wrote in 1911, "The great seaport of San Francisco, with its hundreds of seamen coming and going, and its continuous fortifications and naval stations manned by homeless men, made a special claim on the mother hearts of the WCTU." [36] So extensive was the need in 1884 that Seamen's Union (WCTU) was organized. They gave weekly socials for the sailors, held gospel temperance meetings and kept a library and reading room open.[37]

Chaplain Axton of Ft. Riley appealed to Kansas WCTU when 25,000 soldiers were assigned to Ft. Riley for maneuvers in the summer of 1906. Nearby states joined in financing the WCTU arranged project. A large gospel tent was erected, equipped with a graphaphone and piano. The men came in swarms, using 1000 sheets of letter paper a day and keeping the piano "working overtime." [38]

Senior and junior hostesses were on duty every evening in 1943 at "Town Home," the WCTU Lounge at Greensboro, North Carolina. They served refreshments and made soldiers stationed in the area welcome to the easy chairs, magazines and writing materials provided for their comfort.[39]

The WCTU became an immediate and integral part of the Woman's Committee of the National Council of Defense during World War I. With wheatless days ordered by the Federal Government, they urged "Bake the Barley into Bread and Bar It from the Bar." [40]

Hundreds of thousands of "comfort bags" containing scissors, needles, buttons, were made of khaki cloth for the soldiers, blue denim for the sailors. Nearly $130,000 was donated for war orphans in Europe.[41] $41,473 was contributed for field kitchens and $13,600 for ambulances.[42]

Mrs. Mary Sibbitt of Wichita, Kansas, was given credit for originating the WCTU Cooky Jar in 1924. An eight gallon jar in the Chaplain's tent at Ft. Leavenworth was filled daily for two weeks by the WCTU women of Kansas.[43]

Mrs. Ida B. Wise Smith
National President 1933-1944

The New York Times paid tribute to the WCTU Cooky Jar project in a two-column article in its issue of October 6, 1941. Noting that 27,000 homebaked cookies were consumed by service men at Ft. Dix, in June, 1941, *The Times* reporter commented, "Twenty thousand homemade cookies marching in and out of cooky jars every month are proving a strong attraction for service men off duty at Fort Dix, thanks to New Jersey women who have kept a fresh supply traveling from their kitchens to the camp for the last year." A photo of Mrs. Ella P. Christner, National WCTU Director of the Soldiers and Sailors Department, was printed with the news story.[44]

With the navy on its doorstep, Rhode Island WCTU women not only kept cooky jars filled at three centers in Providence but also three at Westerly and one each at East Greenwich and Newport.[45] Texas WCTU dispensed 1500 dozen weekly from its Austin Cooky Jar and converted their state headquarters into a Red Cross sewing room.

The WCTU still believes that homebaked cookies carry a motherly message of love and concern. In 1960 New Jersey WCTU held its second annual Valentine Cooky Party in the Veterans Hospitals of that state. More than 20,000 cookies were baked, decorated and delivered.[46]

In Southern California in 1963, the WCTU gave over 5000 hours of service. More than 50,000 items such as quilts, scuffies and bed socks were made and distributed.[47]

Many thousands of dollars were raised and expended by the state WCTU's for Red Cross equipment in 1942 and 1943. Missouri purchased two Blood Bank Units and a Clubmobile for use overseas. New York presented a blood bank unit and an ambulance to the Red Cross. Iowa, Pennsylvania, Nebraska, Ohio, Alabama purchased ambulances. Illinois, New Jersey and Virginia supplied money for mobile canteens. Altogether WCTU funds supplied eleven ambulances, five blood bank units, two mobile canteens, two station wagons and a clubmobile.[48]

A unique wartime service sponsored by the WCTU during World War II was the Safety School on Wheels. Capt. James A. W. Killip fitted a 25-foot automobile trailer with devices for testing physical fitness, specifically fitness to drive a motor vehicle. Colorful charts and statistical graphs showing the relationship of alcohol to driving efficiency keyed the entire ensemble to a lesson in Alcohol Education.

Financed by the WCTU, Capt. Killip's colorful caravan was eagerly welcomed by USO Clubs across the country. Parked at a strategic point, it attracted repeated visits from service men and civilians who could not resist personally testing their abilities on the various devices. Trained attendants were always in charge showing films and demonstrating tests. The School travelled fifteen thousand miles in 1942. Hundreds of thousands of service men participated in this diversional and educational program as the WCTU conducted it for more than eight years.[49]

Any report of WCTU cooperation with the Red Cross or military agencies has always included blood donors, Christmas boxes, letters to service men, an enormous amount of knitting and sewing, and cookies, cookies, cookies.

During the Korean War, the WCTU majored in sending natural fruit juices to the American soldiers in Korea. Blanch Pennington, National Director, announced that $42,000 worth of canned fruit juices were sent by the WCTU through regular army channels in 1951.[50]

As the ordeal of the war in Vietnam came to a close, the WCTU effort to let men in service know of their concern and desire to help was evidenced in the thousands of dollars expended for soft drinks to be dispensed to men far from home.[51] Hopefully, the organization may relax its wartime efforts and concentrate on the opportunities in a "Generation of Peace."

Chapter 8

COOPERATION AND CONVENTIONS

When the white ribbon bow, emblem of the Woman's Christian Temperance Union, appeared on the television screen during the early evening network news of the Columbia Broadcasting System on a Sunday evening in August, 1970, millions of TV watchers throughout the United States recognized its significance. The National WCTU, approachng its centennary year in the climate of a permissive America, is known and recognized by its detractors as well as by its supporters. No nationwide network allocates photographers and top commentators to an assignment which is not newsworthy.

The eleven minute telecast included an interview with Mrs. Fred J. Tooze, National President, who reiterated the long time principles of the WCTU and emphasized current activity. A brief trip through Willard House to the background music of the antique music box in Willard parlor, and a session of the Narcotic Education summer school for teachers with Miss Helen M. Allen and Dr. Andrew C. Ivy as lecturers, completed the script.

The forthright and undeviating opposition of the WCTU to the liquor traffic has, on many occasions, caused the organization to be regarded as the spokesman for the "dry" cause. The WCTU's unceasing effort to cope with beverage alcohol and its related problems through education as well as through legislation has consistently attracted the cooperation of the like-minded.

The WCTU has never failed to have a full delegation at the annual meeting of the National Temperance and Prohibition Council in Washington, D.C. The Council bands together twenty or more nationwide organizations for mutual consultation and concerted action. In addition to financial support, the National WCTU has supplied its share of officers and leaders for the Council.

The WCTU is today one of the twenty-seven national organizations holding membership in the National Council of Women. Participation in the Council dates from its origin in 1888 with Frances E. Willard as first president. Several of the later WCTU presidents have served the Council as officers.

A more recent affiliation to which the WCTU has lent every possible support is the Institute of Scientific Studies for the Prevention of Alcoholism, a project of the American Temperance Society. The Institute's outstanding faculty and superior instruction encourage the attendance of WCTU leaders and motivated the National WCTU to offer scholarships for its summer sessions.

Among the other organized groups with which the National WCTU has consistently cooperated either as active participants or fraternal delegates are the Prohibition Party, National Association of Evangelicals, United Church Women, American Business Men's Research Foundation and National Safety Council. Exchanges of materials and counsel have been mutually beneficial.

Worthy of special note is LISTEN magazine, published by Pacific Press. Designed for youth, the timely content and editorial background of the magazine are so attractive that the WCTU has chosen to promote use of LISTEN rather than attempt such a magazine of their own. Kansas WCTU supplies LISTEN subscriptions to every high school in the state and to a number of colleges.[1] Michigan and New Hampshire carry on a similar program.[2]

Intercollegiate Oratorical Contest

Another WCTU activity which depends upon the cooperation of schools, colleges and educational leaders is the intercollegiate oratorical contest. The National contest, initiated in 1955, has stimulated original research on alcohol and its related problems among hundreds of college students in the states which have participated.

Barbara Stigall, Langston University, Langston, Oklahoma, placed first in the 1955 contest at the National WCTU Convention in Long Beach, California. Miss Stigall won the right to represent Oklahoma by competing with students representing eleven other Oklahoma colleges in a preliminary contest. Twelve of Oklahoma's sixteen accredited four-year colleges and universities had entered the WCTU sponsored contest.[3]

Southern California and Kansas have entered contestants in every National contest. Kansas WCTU pioneered the contest plan, holding their first statewide original oration competition in 1948.[4] Seventeen different states have entered the national competition. Many others have sponsored statewide or preliminary contests in individual colleges.

Sponsors agree that the impact of student research is far more far-reaching than its presentation from the contest platform. Southern California noted that 150 students in one college and 123 in another participated in research and basic preparation.[5] A North Carolina college assigned the suggested study as a theme subject for 600 Freshmen. From these essays, six were chosen for development into orations for the local contest.[6]

Equally impressive has been the wide audience before which the contestants are heard. Preliminary contests have often highlighted department convocations or all-student chapel sessions. Local winners have spoken repeatedly before church congregations, high school assemblies and civic clubs.

Orators ranking first in National WCTU contests have been consistent winners in international competition. Harry Smith of Wichita (Kansas), winner of the 1958 National contest, ranked first at the World's WCTU Convention in Mexico City in 1959.[7] David Thompson of Arvada, Colorado, placed first at the World's Convention in Tokyo, Japan, in 1968.[8] Gayle Damarell of Oregon won at Interlaken, Switzerland in 1965. Richard Worley of California North was the winner at the 1971 World's WCTU Convention in Chicago.

They Meet the Press

WCTU activity and leadership have always been newsworthy, attracting attention both favorable and adverse. An Associated Press article which was publicized widely on the 25th anniversary of repeal, December, 1958, showed the tendency of certain elements of the news media to attempt to influence public opinion by implication. William Conway's article, which concerned the WCTU and its president, Mrs. Glenn G. Hays, was friendly, factual and favorable. Hundreds of newspapers printed it as it was written

Mrs. Glenn G. Hays
National President 1953-1959

115

using the photograph Mr. Conway supplied. A few chose to weaken its impact by derogatory headlines and cartoon caricatures.

A similar article syndicated by the Chicago Tribune Magazine of March 21, 1971, was written by Franklynn Peterson. Fairly presenting Mrs. Fred J. Tooze, Mrs. Herman Stanley and Mrs. LAN Nielsen, WCTU officers, with direct quotes, Mr. Peterson could not resist emphasizing what he considered the weaknesses of the organization and its philosophy.[9]

The press has never ignored the Woman's Christian Temperance Union. A National president can expect to see her name in liquor publications almost as frequently as in religious periodicals. An interview with Mrs. Ella A. Boole was one of the leading feature articles in a 1932 *Colliers*. Mrs. Boole, in an election year in which both presidential candidates had refused to support Prohibition, was quoted as saying,, "Liquor doesn't change; it's the same old fight." [10]

Following the Sixty-seventh National Convention in Columbus, Ohio, the *Brewers Journal* headlined a three-page article with "1000 Prohibitionists Attend Convention of Woman's Christian Temperance Union as Ida B. Wise-Smith Retires from Presidency." [11] The same reporter Geo. W. Eads of Anheuser-Busch, Inc., attended the 1955 National convention. His detailed report, five pages in length, illustrated with photographs taken at the scene, appeared in *Modern Brewery Age*. His lead sentence, "Five thousand embattled members of the Woman's Christian Temperance Union assembled in Long Beach, California, city auditorium—," introduced a thorough appraisal of the convention program, exhibits and printed materials. Quoting at length from President Hays' address, he concluded that WCTU women, "never seem to tire or give up hope." [12]

Fifteen years later, a reporter for *Newsweek* wrote of the 1970 National Convention which he attended in Los Angeles, "The WCTU's members and influence are still considerable enough that both California's Governor Ronald Reagan and the state's superconservative Superintendent of Schools, Max Rafferty, agreed to make welcoming addresses on the convention's first day. Because of a last-minute emergency, Reagan had to send a deputy, but Rafferty appeared and gave a talk entitled "The Magic of Education," which ended with a pat on the back for policemen and some strong words against crime on the streets." [13]

Conventions are Highlights

Annual conventions of the National WCTU have always been a highlight of the year, events looked forward to and eagerly attended. Held in different sections of the country they attract first time attendance by members and friends in the area as well as state presidents and other leaders who travel long distances.

Those who come for the first or the thirtieth time are never disappointed. The inspiration of association with women of like minds is worth many, many miles of travel. Attractions which have ranged from elaborate decorations and glamorous pageantry to renowned speakers and momentous decisions have had wide appeal.

The challenge of organizing a working body, developing a constitution and plan of action, discovering leadership, drew Christian women like a magnet during the first years. It was not until the sixth convention that convention programs were outlined in advance. Previous to that a Convention Business Committee arranged them on a day to day basis.[14]

Elaborate, richly decorated banners and pennants were displayed in profusion at Philadelphia in 1885 [15] and in many conventions there-after as state organizations used that means of making an impression. Delaware attracted attention by bringing from Dover a plaque fashioned of 5000 asters, one for each WCTU member enrolled in that state.[16]

Delegates and vistors to the earlier conventions were entertained in private homes in the hostess city. At Philadelphia for the first time, the hostesses arranged for caterers to serve lunch each day at a hall near the convention. This hospitality cost the Philadelphia ladies $600 for the four-day convention.[17]

The extent of attendance—412 registered delegates, 782 registered visitors in 1888 besides those attending only single sessions[18]—soon required commodious meeting places. The Metropolitan Opera House in New York City, second largest auditorium in the country," [19] with its "five galleries, including three tiers of boxes and the dress circle" proved adequate for the 1888 convention except that "an Opera House is not a very good place for a prayer meeting." [19]

The 1891 meeting convened in Tremont Temple, Boston, with a banquet for 3000 ($1 per plate) served in its famed Music Hall. The first World's

White Ribbon Special to Houston, 1930

Convention, a smaller one-day meeting, met in Faneuil Hall, consecrated to the cause of Liberty by James Otis.[20]

In the days when railroads provided the most comfortable and speedy means of travel, special trains were frequently chartered to transport delegates to National conventions. Several lines cooperated in providing and routing a "White Ribbon Special" from Chicago to Seattle for the Twenty-sixth convention in 1899.[21]

Taking advantage of excursion rates from other points, 124 travelers gathered in Chicago to occupy eight "Palace and Tourist Sleeping Cars." Dining cars, baggage cars and a Great Northern Library Car completed the train. Round trip fare was $61.50 plus sleeper charge.

The train, adorned with placards and yards of broad white ribbon, stopped at Fargo, North Dakota, at midnight Saturday and resumed its journey at midnight, Sunday. White Ribbon travelers attended and spoke in Fargo churches on Sunday. Many of the delegates followed the convention by taking a steamship excursion from Seattle to San Francisco and back, two days each way, $24.00[22]

In 1905, railroads throughout eastern, southern and central United States sold round trip tickets for one-way fare plus $1.00 to WCTU members who traveled to Chicago to board the White Ribbon Special to Los Angeles. The response was so great that two trains were required to transport the 500 passengers.[23] The trip was one long series of scenic wonders and special courtesies by communities along the route. Full day stopovers were made at Colorado Springs and Salt Lake City. Delegations with gifts greeted the passengers at each station where a brief stop was made. Following the convention, hundreds of delegates stayed over to be feted with carriage tours, receptions and luncheons in Pasadena, Santa Monica, Whittier, Long Beach and other nearby communities.[24]

It is not unusual for the WCTU to choose a convention site for a specific purpose. In 1939 hundreds of delegates gathered at Rochester, New York, to commemorate the 100th anniversary of the birth of Frances Willard. Sixty-one commercial buses were chartered to take them to her nearby birthplace in the village of Churchville.[25]

The previous year they had convened in San Francisco so that the entire convention could go to Inspiration Point for the dedication of a bronze marker at a point where Frances Willard stood when she envisioned the world-wide future of the WCTU.[26] In 1974, the convention will be held in Cleveland, Ohio, site of the organizing convention in 1874.[27]

In 1917, the WCTU chose to go to Washington, D.C. in an effort to speed action on the Federal Constitutional Prohibition Amendment which was before the U.S. Congress. Patriotism was the theme which was reiterated in speeches, musical selections and decorations. The 906 registered delegates heard the Honorable Jeannette Rankin, Congresswoman from Montana, and Dr. Harvey W. Wiley, Federal Health Commissioner. Mrs. Newton Baker, wife of the Secretary of War, sang a solo; Mrs. Thomas Edison and delegations from the Methodist Board of Temperance and Anti-Saloon League were introduced.

Four Senators and twelve Congressmen attended convention sessions. Secretary of the Navy, Josephus Daniels, and Mrs. Daniels gave a reception in their home.

Ten days later the House of Representatives adopted the Prohibition Amendment by a vote of 282 to 128. The Senate followed suit the next day, 65 to 20.[28]

Pageantry has been a memorable part of many conventions. Youth Night has been a trade mark for the last twenty years when hundreds of youth gather to hold their own supervised convention sessions on the week end. Resourceful leaders have channelled their dramatic and musical abilities into costumed pageants presenting such themes as "Reach Out", "Youth Proud to Abstain", "Lift High the Torch".[29] Eager children invariably "take the cake" as Loyal Temperance leaders march them through hastily rehearsed "Anytown, USA", "Bow White and the Six Senses" or "LTL Echo service." [30]

Carefully staged pageants have been used repeatedly for promotion and commemoration—Pageant Pictures of Fifty Years, 1924; A Star for Every State: A State for every Star, 1942; Turning the Leaves of Our Memory Book, 1954. Clever skits and demonstrations, such as Owl Convention, Indianapolis, 1929, and Fall Fashions, Atlanta, 1956, feature many convention programs.

The Milwaukee Railroad engine was decorated with white ribbon in 1889 when it pulled a special train of 800 delegates from the convention in Chicago to pay respects to Madame Willard at Rest Cottage in Evanston.[31] Again in 1940, delegates went from Chicago to Evanston to dedicate the

State WCTU Presidents, 1969, Lincoln, Nebraska

Library.[32] In 1957 several hundred of the delegates who had attended the National Convention at Madison, Wisconsin, stopped in Evanston to tour Headquarters and enjoy an afternoon party on the lawn.[33]

The respect and deference of public officials and local leaders have been evidenced over and over again by courtesies they have shown. When the National WCTU met in Washington in 1900, six hundred invitations were extended to a White House reception. Both President and Mrs. McKinley stood in the receiving line in the Blue Room to shake hands with the WCTU members.[34]

Governer and Mrs. Northern welcomed Convention delegates to a reception in the Executive Mansion in Atlanta in 1890.[35] Governor Leslie of Indiana and many state officials were present in Indianapolis in 1929 when the WCTU Convention unveiled a Frances E. Willard Memorial tablet in the state capitol building. As the ceremonies proceeded a fleet of airplanes circled above the capitol grounds dropping thousands of flowers which had been donated by Indiana florists.[36]

In 1969, the President of the National WCTU, Mrs. Fred J. Tooze, was invited to Washington to attend an afternoon reception for Distinguished Ladies, where she met Mrs. Richard M. Nixon, Mrs. Spiro T. Agnew and Mrs. Dwight D. Eisenhower. Mrs. Tooze was accorded many courtesies including a reserved seat for the inaugural ceremonies on the Capitol grounds where the newly elected President Nixon took his oath of office.[37]

In addition to being greeted by governors and presidents, WCTU convention delegates have had the privilege of hearing many of the renowned speakers of the country. Among these are William Jennings Bryan, Rev. Edward Everett Hale, Chas. P. Taft, Dr. E. Stanley Jones, Norman Vincent Peale, Daniel A. Poling, Amelia Earhart, Fletcher Dobyns, author of *The Amazing Story of Repeal;* Dr. Lorado Taft, sculptor; Rev. Bob Richards, Olympic pole vault champion; and Roger Babson, statistician.

As the WCTU neared its 100th birthday, evidences of respect for the organization's stability and single-mindedness continued to mount. In October, 1971, elaborate ceremonies at Portland, Maine, marked the gift of the historic Neal Dow Mansion to the Maine WCTU. Built in 1830 by General Neal Dow, father of prohibition and former mayor of Portland, the 17-room landmark will furnish office headquarters for the WCTU and remain a tribute to the principles which the General espoused.[38]

A distinctive ceremony at the National Portrait Gallery of Smithsonian Institution, on February 10, 1972, saw the National WCTU officers presenting a portrait of Frances Willard to the Gallery. The new study of Miss Willard, by artist George Rapp, will be a tourist attraction in the capital city as is the Willard statue in the Capitol rotunda.[39]

Inter-collegiate oratorical contestants who competed for national awards at the 1970 National WCTU Convention in Los Angeles, California.

TREASURERS, 1874-1949

Mrs. Mary B. Ingham
1874-1875

Miss Esther Pugh
1878-1893

Mrs. Abbie F. Leavitt
1875-1878

Mrs. Helen M. Barker
1893-1904

Mrs. Elizabeth P.
Hutchinson
1908-1915

Mrs. Harriett Brand
1904-1908

Mrs. Margaret C.
Munns
1915-1946

Miss Violet T. Black
1946-1952

124

TREASURERS

1952-1973

Mrs. Ernest C. Cameron
1952-1966

Mrs. LAN Nielsen
1966-

125

Chapter 9

THE NEW MORALITY

Permissive attitudes of parents, educators, even religious leaders, made the task of the WCTU more difficult as the organization approached its centennial year. Although millions of homes, of adults and youth, upheld the basic principles of chastity, sobriety and integrity, so many embraced the laxity of the "new morality" that problems related to alcohol and other narcotic drugs multiplied. The drinking automobile driver, drunkenness on aircraft in flight, promotion of drinking by radio and television magnified the menace of liquor.

Thirteen years of National Prohibition materially affected the drinking habits of the drinkers of the United States. Hundreds of thousands insisted on having their liquor during those years. They either patronized bootleggers or concocted home brew. Other hundreds of thousands refrained from drinking after the supply of legal liquor they had cached in their cellars was exhausted.

Very few of the children and youth growing up during those years acquired a taste for alcohol. In spite of the insistence of repealists that prohibition was a challenge to hot-headed youth which drove them to drink, they and everyone else knew that this was the exception rather than the rule. With no advertising and little social pressure to promote casual drinking, the challenge of the speak-easy actually reached only a small percentage of young people.

Abstaining youth, a product of thirteen years of imperfectly enforced Prohibition, were a problem which the liquor interests recognized. Evidence of this recognition appeared, among other places, in an advertisement printed in the November 19, 1932, *Brewing Industry*.[1]

Heading the article were the words, "Half the expected market for beer does not exist today." Its author went on to explain that before prohibition "beer was regarded as a concomitant of a college career." He reasoned that during prohibition "college youth have been poisoning themselves with 'alky,' 'corn,' etc."

He stated, "Not one-tenth of one per cent of the youth in college know what really good American Beer tastes like. They will have to be educated." He proposed, "It should be a cooperative campaign to sell beer, to create a vigorous demand for good legal beer before it can be supplied to them, to make them avid for it. Then when the law makes beer legal, the individual brewers can sell their particular product." [1]

The permissive attitudes which are so integral a part of the new morality are a boon to any campaign which increases sale and consumption of alcoholic beverages. The decade following repeal in 1934 saw the brewers and distillers, all those associated with production and sale of alcoholic beverages, exerting strenuous efforts to regain the market which the prohibition years had decimated. Distillers' sales in million tax gallons had increased only from 68.1 in 1934 to 129.3 in 1943, even though their legal product was sold in 46 states in 1943 as compared to 28 states in 1934. [2]

Home Life Advertising

The best coordinated and most obvious effort to enlist new drinkers and to increase consumption was the national magazine advertising campaign launched by the United States Brewers Foundation in 1947. Postulating that "strong social acceptance is one of the strongest defenses against the Drys," the Brewers "Home Life in America" advertising sought to raise the social standing of beer "by associating it with the home, with nice surroundings, with nice people." [3] Their advertisements, created by the best artists, were perfect in execution.

Their extensive three-year campaign made it clear that "Beer Belongs" everywhere. At the Thanksgiving Dinner as the wholesome gray-haired grandmother proudly places the bronzed turkey on a laden table. In the family living room as the thoughtful mother eases the embarrassment of her daughter's first beau by bringing in beer for all. *Brewery Age* was probably correct when it predicted, "It will be pretty difficult to dislodge an industry that has sold itself to American mothers." [4]

127

Statue of Frances E. Willard
Placed by the state of Illinois
in the Capitol, Washington, D.C.
1905

Congressional Attention

The J. Walter Thompson Company, which handled the Home Life in America advertising, stated its purpose, "The need is to gradually increase the consumption of the present beer drinkers and to win users." [5]

As per capita consumption of distilled liquor increased from .70 gallons in 1935 to 1.65 gallons in 1946,[6] the WCTU joined other concerned organizations in asking Congress to prohibit the transportation in interstate commerce of advertising of alcoholic beverages. Bills were introduced in both the Senate and House of Representatives.

The widespread interest in and growing concern for the invasion of the home by alcoholic beverage advertising was shown by extensive Congressional Hearings. Mrs. D. Leigh Colvin and other proponents, supported the Capper Bill in a 1947 Hearing. Only a few opponents, persons or groups who would be financially hurt by a restriction on liquor advertising, appeared to testify.[7]

But the liquor people were out in force for a Hearing on the same bill in the spring of 1948. Elaborately prepared, they presented an impressive display purporting to show that their advertising did not attempt to increase drinking. Its intent, they argued, was simply to urge a drinking person to choose one brand in preference to another.[8]

Arthur P. Bondurant, vice-president of Glenmore Distilleries Co., Louisville, Kentucky, advanced the same reasoning when he said at a later Hearing, "there is no indicated relation between the value of advertising and total liquor sales." [9]

The "drys," including the WCTU and other cooperating groups, had plenty of evidence to the contrary. As was to be expected, many Congressmen felt that the liquor interests would hesitate to spend millions of dollars for advertising unless they hoped for increased business because of the expenditure.

In 1954, lengthy Hearings were held in both the Senate and House of Representatives. Thirty or more adversaries appeared to support either side of the controversy. Clinton M. Hester, Washington Counsel of the U.S. Brewers Foundation, contradicated previous wet testimony when he said, "Advertising is the life-blood of the manufacture and sale of liquor." [10]

Mr. Hester had been on the staff of the Justice Department of the United

States, presumably had helped write the 21st Repeal Amendment. He seemed to carry weight when he said, "Advertising is the sale, and when you curb advertising by this bill, you would stop the sale of 50 percent of all alcoholic beverages that are sold in the United States today." [11]

Again in 1956, both the House and Senate Committees held extensive Hearings in crowded caucus rooms. Mrs. Glenn G. Hays, Mrs. C. V. Biddle and Miss Elizabeth Smart joined a long list of distinguished proponents in supporting the legislation as they had in 1954.

Appraisal by TAP & TAVERN

Following the 1956 Congressional session, the appraisal of at least one segment of the liquor press appeared in *Tap & Tavern*. "The best that can be said of the past session is that the alcoholic industry was 'saved by the bell.' This may seem a sour comment on the past Congress, in view of the work put in by some committees on technical revisions of the law affecting the alcoholic beverage trades and industry. But the fact is that only the end of the session headed off a major catastrophe in the anti-advertising bill. With an election just around the corner, and the Drys putting local pressure on Congressmen in tight election contests at home, there was little doubt that if time had allowed, an anti-advertising bill might have slipped through.

"This would have muzzled the whole industry, hobbled all the promotion of brands, deprived the industry of much of its value to other fields as a source of revenue, and in short, would have gone a long way to cutting the props from under it. You can look for a revival of this drive next session.

"The same session was ready to pass into law a bill to shut off cocktail service on domestic airlines; the bill did pass the House and only adjournment saved it from possible adoption by the Senate." [12]

Tap & Tavern was correct in its prophecy. Four days were devoted to a Senate Hearing on the Langer Bill, S.582 in the spring of 1958. Among the proponents were Norman Vincent Peale, Mrs. Glenn G. Hays, Dr. Geo. W. Crane and Mrs. Augusta K. Christie. They were well aware that the anti-advertising bills had been buried session after session in the Senate Committee to which they had been referred. Despite extensive Hearings and personal consultations, the Chairman of the Interstate Commerce Committee did not call the bills up for consideration by the entire Committee. Bills do

Mrs. D. Leigh Colvin
National President 1944-1953

not receive the attention of the Senate unless they have been favorably acted upon in the Committee to which they are assigned.

In fairness to Chairman Magnuson, it must be noted that he exerted his very great personal influence in 1961 to prevent the advertising of distilled liquor on the air. And again in 1964, a threat of legislation by Senator Magnuson caused several eastern radio stations to drop their plans for advertising distilled liquor.[13] But no bills on the subject have come before the Senate. It might also be noted that by 1970 per capita consumption of distilled liquor had risen to 1.83 gallons.[14]

Pilots Ask Restriction

While the "drys" were exerting continuing effort to bring about restriction of liquor advertising, another organization, the Airline Pilots Association, was urging legislation which the WCTU could wholeheartedly endorse. Several Congressmen introduced bills to prohibit the serving of alcoholic beverages on aircraft in flight and H.R. 8000, introduced by John Bell Williams of Mississippi, was voted upon and passed by the House on July 25, 1956.[15] The Senate adjourned without considering the legislation.

With the opening of the new Congressional session in January, 1957, three Congressmen and two Senators introduced bills similar to H.R. 8000. It was generally conceded that the legislation would pass if it could get to the floor for vote. The House had shown its support. The burden of proof was on the Senate.

Senator Strom Thurmond of South Carolina was on the committee, the Interstate Commerce Committee, to which his airline bill had been referred. In spite of his continuing effort and that of other supporting senators on the committee, supplemented by the efforts of numerous concerned temperance and civic organizations, the bill was not placed on the Committee agenda for consideration until late June, 1960.

Before it had been called up for Committee discussion and vote, Congress recessed for the Presidential election campaign of 1960. That committee never met again. The obstacles and delay which a few powerful Congressional leaders had been able to marshal had effectively silenced Congress on any legislation which might have been restrictive to the liquor traffic.

Through the 1960's, standards once considered basic were abandoned; ideals vital to the Christian concept were ridiculed. The "new morality"

132

flourished. The impact of drinking and drugs upon the nation and its citizens was regarded with indifference by many.

Such a situation cannot endure forever. The decadence which comes from profligate living eventually takes its toll. Thinking people begin to demand that responsibility accompany freedom.

Factual Evidence

The WCTU, always committed to total abstinence and to any reasonable program designed to minimize the problems related to the use of alcohol and other narcotic drugs, has attempted to assist in the dissemination of factual evidence related to these problems.

When, in 1956, *Pageant* magazine printed "The Big Lie about Moderate Drinking," [16] the National WCTU ordered 30,000 reprints. The twelve-page article headlined information which the WCTU had been emphasizing for years.

"Alcohol is a habit-forming drug.[17] Brain and nervous system cells are the first to be affected by alcohol.[18] Moderate drinking is dangerous.[19] Alcohol is the greatest single cause of insanity." [20]

The *Pageant* article stated forthrightly that brain cells destroyed by alcohol could not be regenerated. Fourteen years after its publication, scientists began to reveal through the general press that even small and infrequent doses of alcohol destroy brain cells, that there is no safe level for drinking.[21] In 1970, Dr. Melvin H. Knisely of the Medical University of South Carolina reported experiments which showed how alcohol deprives the brain of oxygen.

Traffic safety as related to drinking is another area in which facts patiently and persistently presented by the WCTU are now widely accepted and publicized. After thirty years nearly every state legislature has accepted the scientific fact that the percent of alcohol in a motorist's bloodstream can be accurately determined by a simple chemical breath test.

The National Highway Safety Act of 1966 is forcing reluctant states to adopt .10 percent as the presumptive level of intoxication for tested drivers. The National Safety Council mentions .04 percent as the level at which "increased accident causation" is noticeable.[22] The WCTU has consistently advocated that .05 percent be adopted as the presumptive level of intoxication.

Chemical tests protect the innocent as well as incriminate the guilty. Implied consent statutes have been recommended to insure their use. A motorist, in obtaining his license to drive, implies that he will submit to tests if a legal authority calls upon him to do so. In 1957 only four[23] states had adopted implied consent laws. Forty-six states had implied consent statutes in 1970[24] That year a concerted effort appeared to pin the blame on the alcoholic.

"Alcoholics, not social imbibers, cause most deaths on American highways today," said U.S. News & World Report.[25] They were echoing the attitude of Licensed Beverage Industries, Inc. which appeared that same month in paid advertising in some magazines. "Experts agree that the biggest problem on highways is not the social drinker but the chronic alcoholic." [26] One of the experts who did not agree was Dr. E. J. Kelleher, director of the Psychiatric Institute in Chicago, whose study in 1970 "revealed that 80 percent of those convicted of DWI are social drinkers, not alcoholics." [27]

With 30,000 traffic deaths attributed to alcohol each year, lax enforcement and lenient courts are receiving a share of the blame. Judge Raymond K. Berg of Chicago Traffic Court reduced holiday traffic toll by more than one-half at Christmas, 1970, by adopting a policy of sentencing those found guilty of driving while under the influence of liquor to at least seven days in jail and revoking driving licenses for one year.[28]

Evidence Unrecognized?

The legal liquor traffic is probably more firmly entrenched and more influential in America today than it was before National Prohibition. It fits into the uncritical way of life of the new morality.

One must look ahead to suggest that its prosperity and fairly universal acceptance may eventually be its downfall. As a larger and larger proportion of Americans become drinkers, a larger and larger number suffer alcoholism, drink-induced accidents and crime. Eventually drinking may receive the blame it deserves.

After World War I, cigarets became the mainstay of the tobacco industry. Increasing millions, who had shown no interest in other tobacco products, became cigaret smokers. Advertising and promotion devices were designed to win new smokers and to influence other smokers to smoke more. Cigaret smoking became a way of life in America. "Everybody" smoked.

Cigaret advertising was voluminous, virtually unrestrained, carefree. Cigarets brought in billions of dollars in tax revenues.

On January 2, 1971, all advertising of cigarets on radio and television was stopped by the Federal government. The evidence of cigaret contribution to lung cancer and heart disease had become so compelling that it could not be ignored. The widespread use of cigarets had pinpointed their threat to the welfare of mankind.

For the past forty years—since the repeal of National Prohibition—the liquor industry has felt little restriction through the legislative process. Aided by an economy which forces government at any level to grasp for every possible tax source, liquor production and consumption have increased.

Advertising by Licensed Beverage Industries, Inc. in late 1972 repeats a recurrent theme, "You're the people who know there is no harm in liquor itself, but in its abuse." [29] The full-page advertisement details the joys of drinking and concludes, "We, the makers and sellers of distilled spirits, have long urged the responsible use of our products." [29]

Paragraphs which appeared in a liquor trade magazine in mid-1971 reveal the manner in which liquor industry objectives are pursued. "The absence of liquor advertising in television and radio has proved a bonanza for magazines.

"True, there's no law against liquor advertising in the airlanes, but the distillers and the principal networks have forged what amounts to a gentlemen's agreement not to advertise alcoholic beverages in these media, except beer and wine.

"Distillers fear that, if they force the issue of liquor advertising in the airwaves, they might offend the dries, especially that powerful organization funded by religious sects, the Women's Christian Temperance Union, which brought about Prohibition and its concomitant ills. The feeling in the industry is that the WCTU is far from dead and that, if provoked, it could again cause considerable harm.

"That's the reason why the 83-member DSI, the industry watchdog, prohibits even the use of athletes to endorse alcoholic beverage products, on the theory that youngsters would emulate what they see. For the same reason, testimonials on the medicinal values of alcoholic beverages are also frowned upon by the industry." [30]

Members of the United States Congress, Five National WCTU Officers—Mrs. Fred J. Tooze, Mrs. H. F. Powell, Mrs. L. G. Rowley, Mrs. T. Roy Jarrett, Mrs. Glenn G. Hays—and other temperance leaders breakfast in the Senate Dining Room, 1959

The increasingly widespread use of beverage alcohol in America continues to pinpoint the problems it creates. On August 1, 1972, the Federal Government issued eight tough standards for State laws for Traffic safety— No. 8—"Forbid driving by anyone with a blood-alcohol content of .10 percent or more. Refusal to take a breath test for alcohol when requested to do so would be automatic grounds for suspension of a driver's license." [31] Eventual popular rejection of the permissiveness of the new morality will include rejection and restriction of the liquor traffic.

Chapter 10

A HERITAGE TO CLAIM

Women who have been active in the Woman's Christian Temperance Union have invariably had one trait in common—dedication. That has been true not only of the leaders but of those who have given endless hours and effort in local unions. Much of the service rendered, most of the sacrifice offered will go unchronicled because it is unrecorded except in the influence exerted, in the impact made upon lives and upon society in general.

That is the sum total of dedication. And that is the ingredient which has extended the scope and impact of the WCTU far beyond its size and authority.

Only a few present-day WCTU leaders know the name Margaret Keenan Harrais. The service she gave to the temperance cause was not unique but it is revealing of the many opportunities which open for a woman of dedication.

Margaret Keenan was born in Ohio at about the time of the Women's Temperance Crusade. Reared in a "temperance family", she began teaching in Ohio, went on to Idaho, and then to Alaska where, after some years, she became city superintendent of the Fairbanks schools.[1] Also in Alaska, Margaret married Martin Luther Harrais, a miner, and held appointment for many years as U.S. Commissioner for the Third District, which meant acting as coroner and performing marriage ceremonies.[2]

These facts are on the record but Margaret Harrais was continuously concerned that the children in her schools be exposed to principles conducive to good citizenship. She worked closely with the state superintendent of schools to establish a program of scientific temperance instruction. She

138

lost two teaching positions because of her temperance activities in wet communities.

Margaret Harrais sought out opportunities for furthering the cause in which she believed. She was a state officer in Idaho WCTU, president of the Territorial WCTU of Alaska and Chairman of Alaska's Woman's National Committee for Law Enforcement. She was successful in politics and in legislative work.[1]

During her years of strenuous activity and during the years when age limited her, Mrs. Harrais had a larger vision. Realizing the importance of the national organization to any local effort in the temperance cause, she set aside her tithe for temperance in the name of the National WCTU.

For a period of forty years Margaret Harrais used a part of her savings to purchase U.S. Government Bonds for the National WCTU, assuring that on their maturity the contribution she wished to make would serve the temperance cause. Letters which came from her home in Alaska to National WCTU presidents in Evanston revealed her joy in this continuing participation. Her final contribution was large in money, almost $70,000, and enormous in dedication.

The First President

Only nine women have occupied the office of President of the National WCTU during its first 100 years. Many others of equal or greater ability have served in other capacities. All had in common commitment to Christian principle and dedication to a cause. Annie T. Wittenmyer, first president of the National WCTU, set a high standard for those who would follow in that office.

Annie Turner Wittenmyer, who served as National President from 1874 to 1879, was a woman of recognized ability, widely and favorably known for the leadership she had given in the Methodist Church and in humanitarian service during and following the Civil War. Her national reputation and prestige were just what the new organization, untried and inexperienced, needed.

Having been appointed Sanitary Agent for the State of Iowa by the Iowa State Legislature, Mrs. Wittenmyer attracted the attention of the U.S. Surgeon General as she developed special diet kitchens to feed the sick and wounded soldiers of the Civil War. Her work with the Medical Commission

VICE-PRESIDENTS

1874–1894
All State Presidents or
their appointed repre-
sentatives were Vice-
Presidents–at–Large

Mrs. Lillian M. N.
Stevens
1894–1898

Miss Anna Adams
Gordon
1898–1914

Mrs. Ella A. Boole
1914–1925

Mrs. Ida B. Wise Smith
1925–1933

Mrs. D. Leigh Colvin
1933–1944

Miss Mary B. Ervin
1944–1950

Mrs. Glenn C. Hays
1950-1953

VICE-PRESIDENTS

Mrs. C. V. Biddle
1953-1958

Mrs. L. G. Rowley
1958-1959

Mrs. T. Roy Jarrett
1959-

resulted in remarkable improvement in hospital cooking for the army. She had also achieved prominence by originating the plans for the Home Missionary Society of the Methodist Church and as editor of *The Christian Woman.*[3]

Mrs. Wittenmyer dramatized the leadership of Christian women by holding a "Woman's National Camp Meeting" at Ocean Grove, New Jersey. Conducted wholly by women, the thousands who attended heard many powerful women speakers.[4]

Twenty-three state WCTU's, auxiliary to the National, were organized during Mrs. Wittenmyer's administration. She exerted every effort to publicize and sell the organization, speaking at 46 large conventions in a single year, 1875.[5]

Frances E. Willard

The National WCTU was a going concern when Frances Willard became its president in 1879. Her faith in its potential, her willingness to expend herself for a cause and her ability to enlist the cooperation of like minds assured its future.

The breadth of Miss Willard's recognition and influence far exceeds that of any other temperance leader, man or woman. She assumed the presidency of the WCTU at a time when women were emerging as "movers and doers" and in an era when thinking people had recognized and were deeply concerned by the havoc wrought by the use of alcoholic beverages.

The story of her eighteen years as president of the National WCTU is a story of expansion, of reaching out to other groups, of the "Do Everything" policy. It may be taken for granted that Frances Willard, with her magnetic personality and capacity for dedication, would have been an outstanding leader in any age in which she had lived. It remains a fact that the era in which she served—post Civil War, late 19th century—was a period of growing general interest in civic and political reform.

The name Frances Willard was a household word. Not uncommon in the daily press were items such as one which appeared in the *Philadelphia Times* in September, 1885. "When the name of Miss Frances E. Willard was announced and that famous advocate of temperance reform stepped to the front of the platform, the building fairly shook with the storm of applause which greeted her." [6] *The Times* reported that 6000 people had assembled in the Academy of Music Association Hall to hear Miss Willard, who gave one of forty historical addresses at the Centennial Temperance Conference in session, September 23 and 24, 1885.

The white marble statue of Frances Willard placed by the state of Illinois in Statuary Hall in the National Capitol marks a distinction which has been accorded few Americans. No state may place more than two statues. On February 17, 1905, Frances Willard was the first woman so honored. In Miss Willard's Centenary Year, 1939, research revealed nearly 300 memorials bearing her name throughout the United States. Among these were stained glass windows, fountains, parks, schools and hospitals. A dormitory at Northwestern University bears her name as does the Frances E. Willard Memorial Library for Alcohol Research in Evanston.

A willing leader and peerless promoter, Frances Willard left much of the detail of the functioning of the growing organization to her able associates. Caroline Buell of Connecticut, Mary Woodbridge of Ohio, Clara C. Hoffman of Missouri, and others serving as National WCTU officers in those early years, deserve much credit for establishing organization practices which placed the emphasis on state and local unions and formed a broad pattern for their effective participation.

Lillian M. N. Stevens

During its first forty years, the vice president of the National WCTU was named by the president. Frances Willard chose Lillian M. N. Stevens of Maine as her vice president in 1894. So it was that on Miss Willard's death in 1898, Mrs. Stevens stepped into the presidency. Reelected to that office annually for the next fifteen years, she ably demonstrated her ability to fill the assignment. Mrs. Stevens, a tall and stately women, had been a leader in the Maine WCTU from the day it was organized. Her name was synonymous with the temperance cause in all of Maine's struggles to secure and retain constitutional prohibition.

The mistress of a substantial home in Stroudwater, a suburb of Portland, Maine, Lillian Stevens had had her husband's support in giving much of her time and talent to civic affairs. As a member of Maine's National Conference for Charities and Corrections, she helped establish the state industrial school for girls and accomplished many prison reforms. Upon her death the Governor of her native state ordered the flag flown at half mast in recognition of the signal contributions she had made.

Mrs. Stevens neglected none of the duties of a National President—membership, platform, finances, missions—but her chief ability and interest lay in legislation. And legislation designed to restrict the liquor traffic was in vogue. In 1911 she reported that nearly every state had adopted some legislation restrictive of the liquor interests. Seven states had adopted state-wide prohibition. Texans had cast 230,000 votes for consttutional prohibition. Eighty-seven of 110 Utah towns had voted out the saloon.

The most dramatic contest had occurred in her home state. Repeated attempts had been made to repeal constitutional prohibition in Maine. The tireless leadership of Mrs. Stevens was a significant factor in saving the amendment by only 758 votes in 1911. The trauma of that campaign caused Mrs. Stevens to issue her historic proclamation predicting National Prohibition within ten years and to initiate the introduction of Prohibition bills in the United States Congress.[7]

Anna Adams Gordon

Anna Adams Gordon was elected president of the National WCTU upon Mrs. Stevens' death in 1914. Miss Gordon had been closely associated with the national organization for nearly forty years, but had never sought nor been elected to any office.

As companion and private secretary to Frances Willard, as appointed vice-president-at-large during Mrs. Stevens regime, Miss Gordon was thoroughly acquainted with every phase of National WCTU work. She had accompanied Miss Willard on organizing trips which touched every state in the union. She had gone directly from Mrs. Stevens' funeral service to appear before a Congressional Committee which was considering National Prohibition.[8]

Miss Gordon served as president during the years when a chief objective of the National WCTU was realized, 1914-1925. The Eighteenth Amendment became effective January 16, 1920. The temperance movement and the WCTU were riding on the crest of a wave of popular favor. Government officials willingly made themselves available for consultation. Northwestern University in Evanston conferred upon Anna Gordon the honorary degree of Doctor of Humane Letters.

Despite such recognition Miss Gordon was best known for and happiest in her work with children. For fifty years she devoted her musical and literary talent to writing songs and stories for the juvenile work of the WCTU. As Loyal Temperance Legion Secretary of the World's WCTU, she united boys and girls of twenty countries in singing "Saloons, saloons, saloons must go!" Many of her songs are still printed in the LTL Song-book.

Ella A. Boole

When Miss Gordon retired from the presidency in 1925, Dr. Ella A. Boole of New York accepted the office. For eleven years she had been the first vice president to be elected by the WCTU in convention. Mrs. Boole was a woman of discernment and judgment. Her long experience in positions of responsibility and leadership had equipped her for the trying years which faced the WCTU.

During its first fifty years, the Woman's Christian Temperance Union had represented standards and ideals acceptable to a growing segment of American citizens. Religious and educational leaders had unhesitatingly identified themselves with its program and policies. The press generally supported prohibition as the best method for control of the liquor traffic.

Now the trend had changed. Constitutional prohibition was the law of the land, enthusiastically and overwhelmingly ratified by the states. But it was not being enforced. Subtle sabotage was making the Eighteenth Amendment the scapegoat for every ill which afflicted America. The economic depression which had plagued European countries was seeping into the United States. Prohibition was being blamed.

Mrs. Boole, who had held all major offices in New York WCTU, who had served as national administrator for the Women's Home Missionary Societies of the Presbyterian Church, who had been honored with doctor's degrees by her alma mater, Wooster, Ohio, and appointed to its Board of Trustees, was faced with the task of bolstering the organization and reiterating its philosophy. She met the challenge with candor and courage.

Adopting the slogan, "Hold Fast and Go Forward", she urged, "Hold fast to our law, hold fast our membership, hold fast our campaign of education that people may see that obedience to the law will mean America will get full benefit of its prohibition law." She wrote and published *"Give Prohibition Its Chance"*, a book still consulted for its accurate content.

Mrs. Boole was able to rally a membership which had become somewhat apathetic upon the accomplishment of Prohibition. Missionary and

145

White Ribbon recruits and their mothers—a look to the future.

educational programs were increased. The WCTU played a prominent part in international relations, promoting and participating in the first Pan-Pacific Women's Conference in Hawaii. But the advent of Repeal was imminent when Mrs. Boole retired to assume leadership of the World's WCTU.

Ida B. Wise Smith

Her successor, Mrs. Ida B. Wise Smith of Iowa, had been her vice president for eight years. Active in the WCTU, state and national, for more than thirty years, Mrs. Smith was well aware of the devastating effect which repeal could have upon the organization, its membership and its program. Undaunted, she accepted the challenge for a new emphasis, for greater effort.

How well Mrs. Smith succeeded may be gauged by the attention she received in the *Brewers Journal* on her retirement eleven years later. The October 15, 1944, issue of that publication devoted two pages to excerpts from Mrs. Smith's annual address, two pages to a report of the convention at which she spoke and printed the President's Recommendations in full.

The report of George W. Eads gave Mrs. Smith credit for "eleven years of intelligent direction" and suggested that if "thinking brewers" had attended the convention at Columbus and "had seen the more than 1000 delegates and visitors in action, they might have gotten some practical and useful ideas for effective public relations." [9] Mr. Eads added, "Since repeal the W.C.T.U. has collected almost $850,000 of its proposed million dollar educational fund. It has expended much money on films and publicity material of various kinds." [9]

That was exactly the approach Mrs. Smith had made. She launched a program of action centering upon the Frances E. Willard Centenary Year of 1939. It gave new emphasis and greatly expanded the educational work of the WCTU. Visual aids for school use, both motion pictures and filmstrips, were produced for the first time. The scope and attractiveness of printed materials were greatly enhanced. Scientific courses for the training of teachers were originated and a research library was built and dedicated in Evanston.

Ida B. Wise Smith was an ordained minister of the Christian Church, Disciples of Christ. She never made a platform speech without quoting from the Scriptures. She challenged many an audience with her application

of 2nd Chronicles 7:14, "if my people who are called by my name, shall humble themselves and pray, and seek my face, and turn from their wicked ways; then will I hear from heaven, and will forgive their sin, and will heal their land."

Mrs. D. Leigh Colvin

Mamie White Colvin, seventh president of the National WCTU, probably gave the temperance cause first place among her interests for a greater portion of her life than any other leader. Reared in a temperance-oriented home, as were her compatriots, she chose temperance oratory as a major college interest, and married D. Leigh Colvin, president of the Intercollegiate Prohibition Association.

The Woman's Christian Temperance Union early became an acceptable channel for her talent as a speaker and as a platform for her convictions for total abstinence and prohibition. After serving as president of the WCTU of New York, she became vice president of the National WCTU and succeeded Mrs. Smith as president in 1944.

Mrs. Colvin was widely recognized for the depth or her knowledge of temperance history and was often called upon to represent the prohibition viewpoint. She served as chairman of the Law Enforcement Committee of the NYC Federation of Women's Clubs. An active Methodist, she was twice elected to the General Conference of that church. Four American colleges honored her with honorary doctor's degrees—Houghton College of New York, Wheaton College of Illinois, Southwestern College of Kansas and Staley's College of the Spoken Word, Boston.

The New York Christian Advocate quoted "one of the most caustic editors of the wet press" as saying of Mrs. Colvin, "She is embattled womanhood personified: she is one of the most competent women that ever carved out a woman's career in America; in fact, she is one of the most capable women of America."

During Mrs. Colvin's term as president, 1944-1953, with television becoming increasingly common in the homes of America, a number of temperance organizations united in an effort to secure national legislation to ban or limit alcoholic beverage advertising. Mrs. Colvin was called to Washington repeatedly to present the WCTU viewpoint in Congressional Hearings which attracted the best informed witnesses of both the wet and dry forces.

Mrs. Glenn G. Hays

Agitation against alcoholic beverage advertising continued through the 1950's with Mrs. Colvin's successor, Mrs. Glenn G. Hays, appearing at Senate Hearings arranged by Bishop Wilbur E. Hammaker and Miss Elizabeth A. Smart, 1954, 1956 and 1958. The hundreds of concerned spectators who crowded the caucus rooms, the Senators who made it a point to be present and the comments of Washington columnists were evidence that the promotion of drinking through advertising was a matter of nation-wide interest and concern.

Agnes Dubbs Hays of Kansas succeeded to the presidency of the National WCTU in 1953 after serving as state president, national recording secretary and for three years as national vice president. Her Kansas heritage, her family background, her husband's support made the Woman's Christian Temperance Union a natural channel for her aggressive personality.

Quickly aware of the need for unity of effort and for cooperation among like-minded groups, Mrs. Hays originated plans for a combined effort "to reach into every age and interest group with authentic and impelling information on the relationship of alcoholic beverages to the problems of the day" [10] The wholehearted support of staff members and state leaders successfully promoted her "Eighty More in '54' " and "Divide to Multiply" emphases.

The National Intercollegiate Oratorical Contest was launched, a Temperance Sermon Contest won participation by full time ministers in thirty-nine states and resulted in the publication of a book, "The Christian Case for Abstinence." Publishing House sales of printed materials doubled those of previous years.

Many opportunities to speak and write about the WCTU came to Mrs. Hays through her church, Disciples of Christ, and other religious and civic organizations. On the 25th anniversary of repeal, December, 1958, she was called to New York to appear on the widely-viewed "Today" show.

Mrs. Fred J. Tooze

Active participation of WCTU leaders in the National Council of Women, the National Safety Council and the National Temperance and Prohibition Council has been the rule. The WCTU has given its enthusiastic support to the Institute of Scientific Studies for the Prevention of Alcoholism

Mrs. Fred J. Tooze
National President 1959-

since its opening session in 1951. Mrs. Colvin, Mrs. Hays and Mrs. Tooze, the ninth president of the National WCTU, have lectured in its sessions and served on its Boards.

Like her predecessors, Ruth Tibbits Tooze of Oregon was reared in a temperance family and held a series of WCTU offices, including president of Oregon WCTU; National recording and corresponding secretary, before becoming National president in 1959. She joined the WCTU shortly after marriage to Fred J. Tooze when her husband brought her a membership card to sign.

Mrs. Tooze has been active in her church, the Baptist, and has served on a number of its commissions as well as in official capacities in a number of social action conferences. She was appointed by the governor to the Oregon Mother Committee to select the Oregon Mother of the Year.

Promotion of the "Hour of Social Freedom" was a highlight early in the presidency of Mrs. Tooze. Gratifying public service cooperation from more than 100 television stations enabled the WCTU to fill thousands of requests for attractive recipe booklets. Response to the Pepsi Project which supplied more than $69,000 for soft drinks for service men in Vietnam was widespread and heartening.[11] Production of visual aids continued to demand a large portion of the WCTU educational budget with new subjects including narcotic drugs in addition to alcohol.

Mrs. Tooze was able to take extensive advantage of television as Mrs. Smith and Mrs. Colvin had of radio. Among the most popular telecasts were a WBBM feature showing the National President concocting and serving a non-alcoholic Christmas drink[12] and the widely viewed CBS network story of the WCTU in August of 1970.

The Press continued to find the Woman's Christian Temperance Union and its president newsworthy as the organization approached its 100th year. On the fiftieth anniversary of Prohibition, January 16, 1970, the *Wall Street Journal* devoted a front page column to an interview with Mrs. Tooze and concluded that the WCTU "was the first successful attempt to marshal the ranks of Protestantism against the liquor traffic." [13] *The Saturday Evening Post* of March 11, 1967, devoted five pages to a profusely illustrated article on the Woman's Christian Temperance Union.

The Names Are Legion

Many other leaders are recognized all too briefly in the pages of this book. Their stature equals that of Mrs. Nelle G. Burger, powerful civic leader in Missouri; Sergeant Violet Hill Whyte, who served with distinction on the Baltimore Police Force for 25 years; Mrs. Culan V. Biddle, whose constant devotion to the WCTU so magnified its influence in Tennessee and all of the South.

An entire book could be written about the achievements and contribution of dozens of others—Mrs. Augusta K. Christie, WCTU president and civic leader who served her state, Maine, in both its assembly and senate; Mrs. Margaret C. Munns, who served as National Treasurer from 1915 to 1946 and to whom the organization owes its stable financial pattern; Mrs. T. Roy Jarrett of Virginia who was president of the World's WCTU for nine years; Miss Bertha Rachel Palmer, who placed the alcohol education program of the WCTU upon an acceptable scientific basis.

Perhaps the record of leadership in the National Woman's Christian Temperance Union is best defined by the words which closed a 1954 convention address—

"Our heritage is the richer because it comes not only from our leaders but from every one of those in the ranks who by their steadfastness made a plan emerge from an idea. Our heritage never fails because the present need calls for each new generation to build upon the principles of the past." [14]

APPENDIX

Chapter One

1. Historic Sites Act of 1935
2. *Union Signal,* Feb. 12, 1966, P. 9
3. NORTON with Willard, *A Great Mother,* 1894, P. 18
4. ibid. P. 11
5. ibid. P. 21
6. WILLARD, *A Classic Town,* 1891, P. 45
7. ibid. P. 45
8. ibid. P. 25
9. ibid. frontispiece quotes charter
10. ibid. P. 166
11. *Evanston Review,* Jan. 11, 1964
12. WILLARD, *A Classic Town,* 1891, P. 175
13. *Evanston Review,* Oct. 3, 1963
14. ibid. Jan. 8, 1942
15. statement, representative Evanston Jr. Chamber of Commerce Jan. 1969
16. *The Daily Northwestern,* Jan. 5, 1972, P. 1
17. ibid.
18. NORTON, A *Great Mother,* P. 64

Chapter Two

1. *Union Signal,* Dec. 20, 1900, P. 3
2. *Annual Report,* 1901, P. 88
3. *Union Signal,* Nov. 28, 1901, P. 3
4. *Annual Report,* 1900, P. 161
5. ibid. 1903, P. 120
6. ibid. 1903, P. 98-100
7. *Union Signal,* Nov. 24, 1910, P. 7
8. ibid. May 25, 1922, P. 5
9. Signed appraisal form, dated May 25, 1920
10. *The American Home,* February, 1936
11. *Union Signal,* Oct. 30, 1924, P. 7
12. Letter of Mrs. Walter Crowell, dated Sept. 6, 1962
13. Typed list, marginal notes, Mrs. A. L. Jones, Cedar Rapids, Iowa, 91 pages
14. *Union Signal,* Feb. 10, 1968, P. 8
15. TYLER, *Where Prayer & Purpose Meet,* 1949, P. 82
16. ibid. P. 83
17. *Union Signal,* Feb. 13, 1954, P. 10
18. *Evanston Review,* Sept. 28, 1939

19. *Union Signal,* Sept. 4, 1954, P. 5
20. ibid. Sept. 3, 1955, P. 5
21. ibid. May 11, 1957, P. 5
22. ibid. June 11, 1960, P. 5
23. ibid. Dec. 9, 1961, P. 5
24. Centennial brochure and tile
25. *Union Signal,* Feb. 12, 1966, P. 8
26. ibid. Feb. 12, 1966, P. 3
27. ibid. Feb. 13, 1954, P. 10

Chapter Three

1. TYLER, *Where Prayer & Purpose Meet,* 1949, P. 7
2. STEVENSON, *Brief History of the WCTU,* 1907, P. 7
3. HOWARD, *The Woman's Crusade,* P. 3
4. ibid. P. 6
5. ibid. quoting *Fredonia Censor,* Dec. 17, 1873
6. WILLARD, *Glimpses of Fifty Years,* P. 341
7. CHERRINGTON, *Standard Encyclopedia of the Alcohol Problem,* vol. 6 P 2905
8. STEVENSON, *Brief History of the WCTU,* P. 8
9. CARPENTER, *Crusade at Washington Courthouse,* P. 104
10. HOWARD, *Women's Crusade,* quoting *Fredonia Censor,* Dec. 17, 1873, P. 5
11. MOTHER STEWART, *Memories of the Crusade,* P. 87
12. CARPENTER, *Crusade at Washington Courthouse,* P. 125
13. TYLER, *Where Prayer & Purpose Meet,* P. 24 & P. 20
14. *Minutes* of National WCTU Convention, 1874, P. 6
15. CAYLOR, *Matchless Machine,* 1949
16. WILLARD, *History of the Woman's National WCTU,* 1876
17. STEVENSON, *Brief History of the WCTU,* P. 46
18. *Union Signal,* Nov. 16, 1905, P. 7
19. ibid. Oct. 21 and 28, 1915
20. GORDON, *Women Torchbearers,* 1924, P. 182
21. *Union Signal,* May 1, 1954, P. 3
22. *Women Torchbearers,* P. 223
23. STANLEY, *Growth Progress*
24. *Brief History of the WCTU,* P. 53

Chapter Four

1. TYLER, *Where Prayer & Purpose Meet,* 1949, P. 37
2. *Brief History of the WCTU,* P. 12
3. ibid. P. 15
4. *Union Signal,* Sept. 13, 1958, P. 6
5. CHERRINGTON, *Standard Encyclopedia of the Alcohol Problem,* Westerville, O. 1926

6. JOHNSON, *The Federal Government and the Liquor Traffic,* 1910
7. DOBYNS, *The Amazing Story of Repeal,* 1940, P. 216
8. Maine, Minnesota, Rhode Island, Massachusetts, Vermont, Michigan, Connecticut, Indiana, Delaware, Iowa, Nebraska, New York, New Hampshire, COLVIN, *Prohibition in the United States,* Doran & Co., 1926, P. 47
9. DOBYNS, *The Amazing Story of Repeal,* 1940, P. 221
10. ibid. P. 225
11. ibid. P. 227
12. ibid. P. 222
13. *Annual Report,* National WCTU, 1901, P. 318
14. *Union Signal,* Nov. 9, 1911, President's Address
15. Maine, Kansas, North Dakota, Oklahoma, Georgia, North Carolina, Mississippi, Tennessee, *Women Torchbearers,* P. 133-134
16. HAYS, *White Ribbon in the Sunflower State,* 1953, P. 58
17. STUBBS, Governor of Kansas, *Facts Proved by Figures.*
18. *Union Signal,* Aug. 22, 1912, P. 3
19. ibid. Mar. 16, 1911, P. 5
20. ibid. July 25, 1912, P. 5
21. ibid. June 15, 1911, P. 3
22. DOBYNS, *The Amazing Story of Repeal,* P. 242
23. ibid. P. 244
24. ibid. P. 252
25. ibid. P. 388
26. BOOLE, *Give Prohibition Its Chance,* P. 162
27. DOBYNS, *The Amazing Story of Repeal,* P. 255
28. ibid. P. 370
29. ibid. P. 373
30. ibid. P. 3
31. ibid. P. 12
32. ibid. P. 23—Hearings before a Subcommittee of the Judiciary, U. S. Senate, 71st Congress, 2nd session, P. 4167.
33. ibid. P. 380
34. *Brewers Journal,* Oct. 15, 1944, P. 36

Chapter Five

1. *Brewing Industry,* Nov. 19, 1932
2. ibid.
3. Iowa, California, Colorado, Florida, Georgia, Minnesota, Mississippi, North Dakota, South Dakota.
4. *Union Signal,* Jan. 23, 1954, President's Page
5. *Annual Report,* 1969, P. 93
6. ibid. 1965, P. 82
7. ibid. 1959, P. 110
8. TYLER, *Where Prayer & Purpose Meet,* P. 239

9. YTC Plan of Work, Mar. 13, 1943
10. MORT, *Origin and History of Temperance Sundays,* P. 1
11. ibid. P. 3
12. *Bethany Quarterly,* Christian Board of Publication, P. 30-45
13. TYLER, *Where Prayer and Purpose Meet,* P. 156
14. STANLEY, *Growth Progress,* Pamphlet, 1928 item.

Chapter Six

1. TYLER, *Where Prayer & Purpose Meet,* P. 26
2. GORDON, *Women Torchbearers,* P. 15
3. TYLER, *Where Prayer & Purpose Meet,* P. 33, quoted
4. GORDON, *Beautiful Life of Frances E. Willard,* 1898, P. 106
5. *Brief History of the WCTU,* P. 114
6. ibid. P. 116
7. ibid. P. 114
8. *Union Signal,* Nov. 9, 1899, P. 13
9. *Brief History of the WCTU,* P. 116
10. ibid. P. 3
11. ibid. P. 116
12. *Union Signal,* Dec. 18, 1954, P. 3, quoted
13. ibid. Mar. 19, 1938, P. 7
14. ibid. July 17, 1954, President's Page
15. ibid. Sept. 28, 1957, P. 5
16. ibid. July 17, 1954, & June 5, 1954
17. ibid. Apr. 25, 1960, P. 3
18. ibid. Feb. 24, 1962, P. 15
19. ibid. April, 1970, President's Page
20. *Promoter,* Feb. 1972
21. *Annual Report,* 1939, P. 214
22. *Union Signal,* Mar. 10, 1956, President's Page
23. ibid. Apr. 27, 1968, P. 15
24. ibid. Dec. 27, 1958, President's Page
25. Letter, Tooze to Hays, Sept. 25, 1970
26. Records, Public Relations Counsel, Caylor
27. WILLARD, *Glimpses of Fifty Years,* 1889, P. 695
28. *Annual Report,* 1889, Appendix, P. 163
29. GORDON, *Beautiful Life of Frances E. Willard,* 1898
30. GORDON, *Women Torchbearers,* 1924
31. BOOLE, *Give Prohibition Its Chance,* Fleming H. Revell Co., 1929
32. TYLER, *Where Prayer & Purpose Meet,* Signal Press, 1949
33. *Union Signal,* Mar. 5, 1955, P. 4
34. ibid. Oct. 1, 1955, P. 5
35. Letter, Association Press to Hays, Apr. 8, 1971
36. *Union Signal,* June 5, 1937, P. 10

157

37. ibid. Jan. 9, 1954, P. 8
38. ibid. Mar. 5, 1955, P. 5
39. ibid. July 17, 1954, P. 3
40. ibid. June 18, 1955, P. 5
41. ibid. June 5, 1954, Pres. Page
42. ibid. May 1, 1954, Pres. Page
43. *Modern Brewery Age,* Sept. 1955, P. 45
44. *Annual Report,* 1886, Appendix, P. 163
45. ibid. 1888, P. 230
46. *Union Signal,* Nov. 20, 1924, P. 11
47. *Voice of Song,* P. 7
48. ibid. P. 29
49. ibid. P. 11
50. ibid. P. 21

Chapter Seven

1. *Union Signal,* Mar. 25, 1967, P. 5
2. ibid. June 22, 1968, P. 3
3. *Annual Report,* 1971, P. 40
4. *Union Signal,* July, 1970, P. 23
5. CAYLOR, *Matchless Machine,* P. 13
6. TYLER, *Where Prayer & Purpose Meet,* P. 86
7. GRAHAM, *A History of Sixty Years Work,* P. 71
8. *Annual Report,* 1927, P. 108
9. National Treasurer's Report.
10. *Union Signal,* Feb. 22, 1958, P. 9
11. ibid. Feb. 20, 1960, P. 4
12. Tooze letter dated Aug. 20, 1970
13. HAYS, *White Ribbon in the Sunflower State,* P. 31
14. WELDIN, *Background and History of Delaware WCTU,* P. 19
15. WCTU letter, Marion Co. Indiana, 1971
16. *Union Signal,* Nov. 2, 1889, P. 10
17. letter, New Hampshire WCTU President, Mrs. Ernest Campbell, Sept. 13, 1971
18. *WCTU Champion,* Iowa, Oct. 1, 1968, Harriette G. McCullough
19. data supplied by Nebraska WCTU, Sept. 1971
20. *Annual Report,* 1892, P. 247 and Mrs. Lucretia Acker
21. *A History of WCTU of North California*
22. Vanderburgh Co. WCTU History
23. SPENCER, *History, WCTU of N. California,* 1911, P. 119
24. MIMS, *Recorded History of South Carolina WCTU,* P. 25
25. SPENCER, *History, WCTU of N. California,* 1911, P. 118
26. Letter, Harris to Hays, Dec. 8, 1958
27. *Alabama White Ribbon,* May, 1967

28. brochure, *History & Program, Gateway,* Jefferson Co. Chamber of Commerce, Birmingham
29. brochure, *Children's Farm Home,* Corvallis, Oregon
30. brochure, *The Frances E. Willard Club,* Oakland, Calif.
31. WCTU Directory, District of Columbia, 1901, Clara Blystone
32. HAMILTON, *Story of Alabama WCTU, 1884-1959,* P. 9
33. HAYS, *White Ribbon in the Sunflower State,* P. 49-50
34. *Union Signal,* Oct. 1, 1955, P. 9
35. ibid. Sept. 22, 1956, P. 8-9
36. SPENCER, *History, WCTU North & Central California,* P. 121
37. ibid. P. 122
38. HAYS, *White Ribbon in the Sunflower State,* P. 45
39. *Union Signal,* Jan. 8, 1944, P. 10
40. TYLER, *Where Prayer & Purpose Meet,* P. 169
41. ibid. P. 169
42. GORDON, *Women Torchbearers,* P. 131
43. HAYS, *White Ribbon in the Sunflower State,* P. 47
44. *Union Signal,* Oct. 25, 1941, P. 5
45. ibid. May 16, 1942, P. 4-5
46. ibid. Apr. 9, 1960, P. 4
47. *Victories of Four Decades,* Southern California, P. 55
48. *Union Signal,* Mar. 11, 1944, P. 11
49. ibid. July 1, 1944, P. 24
50. *Annual Report,* Convention Minutes, 1951, P. 156
51. First paragraphs this chapter

Chapter Eight

1. *Union Signal,* December, 1970, P. 10
2. ibid. P. 11
3. ibid. Aug. 7, 1955, P. 9
4. *Annual Report,* Kansas WCTU, 1948
5. *Union Signal,* Aug. 7, 1955, P. 10
6. ibid. Sept. 8, 1956, P. 10
7. ibid. Nov. 14, 1959, P. 5
8. ibid. June 22, 1968, P. 5
9. *Chicago Tribune Magazine,* Mar. 21, 1971, P. 17-22
10. *Union Signal,* Nov. 12, 1932, P. 9, quoting *Colliers,* Nov. 5, 1932
11. *Brewers Journal,* Oct. 15, 1944, P. 36-38
12. *Modern Brewery Age,* Sept. 1955, P. 45-49
13. *Newsweek,* Sept. 21, 1970, P. 84
14. *Brief History of the WCTU,* P. 17
15. WILLARD, *Glimpse of Fifty Years,* lithograph, P. 156
16. *Union Signal,* Nov. 12, 1885, P. 2
17. ibid. P. 3

18. ibid. Nov. 8, 1888, P. 8
19. ibid. P. 2
20. ibid. Oct. 29, 1891, P. 5
21. TYLER, *Where Prayer & Purpose Meet,* P. 149
22. *Union Signal,* Nov. 16, 1899, P. 10
23. ibid. Oct. 26, 1905, P. 2
24. ibid. Nov. 30, 1905, P. 2
25. *Annual Report,* 1939, P. 25
26. ibid. 1938, P. 32
27. ibid. 1971
28. *Union Signal,* Dec. 20, 1917, P. 7
29. *Annual Reports,* 1971, 1959, 1965
30. *Annual Reports,* 1958, 1971, 1940
31. *Union Signal,* Nov. 21, 1889, P. 1
32. ibid. Aug. 24, 1940, P. 2-3
33. ibid. July 13, 1957, P. 11
34. ibid. Dec. 27, 1900, P. 10
35. ibid. Nov. 27, 1890, P. 11
36. ibid. Oct. 12, 1929, P. 6
37. ibid. Feb. 8 and Feb. 20, 1969, P. 3 & 5
38. ibid. Dec. 1971, P. 3
39. Invitation & program, Smithsonian National Portrait Gallery

Chapter Nine

1. *Union Signal,* Sept. 23, 1961, P. 6, reprint of *Brewing Industry* ad, Nov. 19, 1932
2. *Facts Book,* Licensed Beverage Industries, Inc. 1965, P. 34
3. *Policy & Purpose of the National Magazine Advertising,* brochure, U.S. Brewers' Foundation, reported to Bd. of Directors at Chicago meeting, Mar. 12, 1947
4. *Brewery Age,* Feb. 1936, P. 32
5. *A Review of the Economic Situation of the Brewing Industry,* March, 1947, quoted in *Report of Senate Hearing on S. 3294, Langer Bill,* 1954, P. 60
6. *Facts Book,* Licensed Beverage Industries, Inc., 1965, P. 34
7. *Hearing Report,* Interstate Commerce Committee, U.S. Senate, May 12-13, 1947
8. *Hearing Report,* April 21-22, 1948
9. *Report of House Hearing, Bryson Bill, No. 1227,* May 19-25, 1954, P. 427
10. ibid. P. 148
11. ibid. P. 147
12. *Tap & Tavern,* Aug. 6, 1956, quoted in Union Signal, Sept. 8, 1956, P. 6
13. *Union Signal,* May 9, 1964, P. 6-7
14. *Annual Statistical Review,* Distilled Spirits Institute, 1970, P. 43
15. *Union Signal,* Aug. 11, 1956, P. 6

16. *PAGEANT*, February, 1956, P. 148-161
17. ibid. P. 152
18. ibid. P. 150
19. ibid. P. 153
20. ibid. P. 153
21. *Reader's Digest*, June, 1970, P. 65
22. *Getting the Alcohol Story to the People*, brochure, National Safety Council, 1970
23. New York, Kansas, Utah, Idaho
24. *U.S. News & World Report*, July 6, 1970 P. 25
25. ibid. P 24
25. ibid. P. 24
26. *Newsweek*, July 27, 1970
27. *Chicago Tribune*, Jan. 14, 1971
28. ibid.
29. *U. S. News & World Report*, Aug. 7, 1972, P. 77
30. *BEV Executive*, July 1, 1971, P. 4
31. *U.S. News & World Report*, Aug. 14, 1972, P. 31

Chapter Ten

1. *Standard Encyclopedia of the Alcohol Problem*, V. 3, P. 1184
2. *Union Signal*, Aug. 16, 1941, P. 5
3. WILLARD, *Woman & Temperance*, Park Publishing Co. 1883, P. 160-164
4. ibid. P. 165
5. GORDON, *Women Torchbearers*, 1924, P. 15
6. *Union Signal*, Oct. 8, 1885, P. 2, quoted
7. ibid. Nov. 9, 1911, P. 5
8. DEANE, *Anna Adams Gordon, A Story of Her Life*, P. 19
9. *Brewers Journal*, Oct. 15, 1944, P. 34-35
10. TYLER, *What Is the WCTU?*, P. 15
11. *Annual Reports*, National WCTU, 1969, 1970, 1971
12. *Union Signal*, Jan. 23, 1965
13. *Wall St. Journal*, Jan. 16, 1970, P. 1
14. *Union Signal*, Sept. 18, 1954, Hays address, P. 4

National WCTU Roster, 1972-1973

General Officers

Mrs. Fred J. Tooze, president
Mrs. T. Roy Jarrett, vice-president
Mrs. Herman Stanley, promotion secretary
Mrs. LAN Nielsen, treasurer
Mrs. J. K. W. Miller, recording secretary

Honorary President

Mrs. Glenn G. Hays

Branch Executive Directors

Youth Temperance Council, Miss Rosalita Leonard
Loyal Temperance Legion, ...

National Bureaus

Legislation, Mrs. Marian B. S. Crymes, Representative
Narcotic Education, Miss Helen M. Allen, Consultant
Public Relations, National officers, Mrs. Marie Caylor, Counsel

Department Directors

Christian Outreach, Mrs. Cleo Parrish
Citizenship, Mrs. Donald A. Johnson
Education, Mrs. Olive Forbes
Home Protection, Mrs. Richard Miller
Legislation, Mrs. J. E. Dillard
Projection Methods, Mrs. Kermit Edgar
Public Relations, Mrs. A. F. Groom
Social Service, Mrs. Cecil Roberts

Special Field Service

Executive Secretary, Mrs. Herman Stanley
Mrs. Clara R. Ports, Latin American
Mrs. Violet Hill Whyte, Special Assignment

Members Emeritus

Rev. Mrs. Emma A. Arnold; Mrs. Ethel Bliss Baker; Miss Estelle Bozeman; Mrs. Augusta Christie; Miss Helen G. H. Estelle; Mrs. Paul Halladay; Mrs. Robert McPherson McDougall; Mrs. Blanche Pennington; Mrs. Ruby Lane Railsback; Miss Lenadell Wiggins.

State Presidents Through the Years

ALABAMA: Mrs. L. C. Woodruff, 1884-85; Mrs. E. P. Bryce, 1885-88; Mrs. W. L. Stratford, 1888-89; Mrs. J. Morgan Smith, 1889-97; Mrs. M. L. Spencer, 1897-1904; Mrs. Mary T. Jeffries, 1904-06; Mrs. C. M. Nullan, 1906-07; Mrs. J. B. Chatfield, 1907-12; Mrs. A. K. Wiesel, 1912-18; Mrs. Mary T. Jeffries, 1918-30; Mrs. Lamar Smith Slaton, 1930-37; Mrs. I. S. McAdory, 1937-47; Mrs. Eunice Hall Sisson, 1947-1949; Mrs. J. E. Dillard, 1949-1970; Mrs. Ira Pegues, 1970-

ALABAMA #2: Mrs. C. C. Boothe 1886-1889; Mrs. Booker T. Washington, 1889-1900; Mrs. J. R. England, 1901-1903; Mrs. A. W. Plump, 1945-1956

ALASKA: Mrs. Susan S. Winans, 1888-1889; Mrs. John G. Brady, 1889-1898; Mrs. S. E. Shorthill, 1899-1909; Mrs. Frances T. Pederson, 1909-1911; Mrs. Margaret B. Platt, 1911-1912; Mrs. Cornelia Templeton Hatcher, 1912-1918; Mrs. Lucy R. Spaeth, 1918-1920; Mrs. Cornelia Hatcher, 1921-1924; Mrs. Margaret Keenan Harrais, 1924-1941; Mrs. Harold C. Newton, 1941-1943; Mrs. Ruth E. Stahr, 1943-1947; Mrs. Earl Smith, 1949-1951; Mrs. Earl C. Chandler, 1951-1960; Mrs. J. E. Brazil, 1962-1964;

ARIZONA: Mrs. L. C. Hughes, 1883-94; Mrs. N. K. Watrous, 1894-95; Mrs. M. B. White, 1895-98; Mrs. A. W. Buckley, 1898-1900; Mrs. Pamelia Otis, 1900-01; Mrs. Imogen LaChance, 1901-12; Mrs. Harriet Beckley, 1912-14; Mrs. Imogen LaChance, 1914-23; Mrs. Leora Lobban Brewer, 1923-26; Mrs. F. B. Stevens, 1926-38; Mrs. Mary N. Pulsifer, 1938-43; Mrs. J. T. Hartman, 1943-1952; Miss Lilian Crandell, 1952-1960; Mrs. S. O. Redacre, 1961-1964; Mrs. Myrtle Molland, 1965-1966; Mrs. Anna Kennedy, 1967-1970; Major Mrs. Gerald Hill, 1971-1972; Mrs. L. G. Rowley, 1972-

ARIZONA (*Sojourner Truth*): Mrs. Amelia Thompson, 1949-1959;

ARKANSAS: Mrs. Annie Jones, 1879-80; Mrs. R. L. Dodge, 1880-82;

Mrs. M. A. Cornelius, 1882-84; Mrs. L. M. Chase, 1884-91; Mrs. T. A. Dunlap, 1891-93; Mrs. S. K. Hart, 1893-94; Mrs. Fannie L. Chunn, 1894-97; Mrs. Mildred Dorsey, 1897-1902; Mrs. Lulu A. Markwell, 1903-12; Mrs. Minnie U. Rutherford, 1912-24; Mrs. Jennie Carr Pittman, 1924-28; Mrs. H. M. Cooley, 1928-29; Mrs. L. B. Crenshaw, 1929-32; Mrs. Cora H. Gillespie, 1932-35; Mrs. N. F. Cooledge, 1936-37; Mrs. May C. Crouse, 1937-43; Mrs. Lewis S. Talley, 1943-46; Mrs. May C. Crouse, 1946-1951; Mrs. J. M. Spicer, 1951-1959; Mrs. Walter Jackson, 1960-1965; Mrs. Richard Nelson, 1966-

ARKANSAS *(Frances W. Harper)*: Mrs. F. C. Potter, 1897-1902; Mrs. Josephine I. Harris, 1902-04; Mrs. Josephine H. Pankey, 1904-05; Mrs. Ida J. Young, 1909-14; (Peterson Union) Mrs. M. R. Stevens, 1915-1921;

CALIFORNIA (North): Mrs. G. S. Abbott, 1880-81; Mrs. P. D. Browne, 1881-82; Mrs. E. H. Gray, 1882-83; Mrs. P. D. Browne, 1883-85; Mrs. S. J. Churchill, 1885-87; Mrs. R. R. Johnston, 1887-91; Mrs. B. Sturtevant-Peet, 1891-1907; Mrs. Sara J. Dorr, 1907-21; Mrs. Addie Garwood Estes, 1921-28; Mrs. Anna A. Pettit, 1928-30; Mrs. Louise J. Taft, 1930-43; Mrs. Ida A. Stine, 1943-1951; Mrs. Nellie Miller, 1951-1966; Mrs. Eila Parker, 1966-1972; Mrs. Cynthia Nelson, 1972-

CALIFORNIA (South): Miss Martha Hathaway, 1883-85; Mrs. Olive Bird, 1885-86; Mrs. Lucy Drew Moore, 1886-88; Mrs. Sophia A. Keyes, 1888-89; Mrs. N. J. Button, 1889-94; Mrs. Mary E. Garbutt, 1894-95; Mrs. N. J. Button, 1895-97; Mrs. Mary A. Kenney, 1897-1902; Mrs. Emma Cash (Clapp), 1902-06; Miss Gabrella T. Stickney, 1906-08; Mrs. Hester T. Griffith (Miller), 1908-12; Mrs. Lucy Blanchard, 1912-15; Mrs. Stella B. Irvine, 1915-20; Mrs. Helen M. Stoddard, 1920-21; Mrs. Eva C. Wheeler, 1921-43; Mrs. Lena Marie Bratton, 1943-46; Mrs. Eva Wheeler Randall, 1946-47; Mrs. Jennie Ray Thompson, 1947-1953; Mrs. Ruth Gates Miller, 1953-1962; Mrs. Lydia A. Wood, 1962-1966; Mrs. Zola M. Meek, 1966-

COLORADO: Mrs. Kittie Thompson, 1879-80; Mrs. Mary F. Shields, 1880-87; Mrs. Kittie Thompson, 1887-90; Mrs. Eva Higgins, 1890-95; Mrs. Mary Jewett Telford, 1895-99; Mrs. Antoinette Arnold Hawley, 1899-1904; Mrs. Adrianna Hungerford, 1904-42; Mrs. Henry Bruce Teller, 1942-1956; Mrs. Anna S. Caldwell, 1956-1960; Mrs. Clarissa Rasmussen, 1960-1967; Mrs. Lorin Lindstrom, 1967- 1971; Mrs. Ethel R. Cook, 1971-

CONNECTICUT: Mrs. H. B. Brown, part of year 1875; Miss Ellen

C. Barnett, 1875-76; Mrs. Mary A. Stone, 1876-79; Miss Maria Stanton, 1879-81; Mrs. Maria C. Treadwell, 1881-83; Mrs. Cornelia B. Forbes, 1883-1904; Mrs. Caroline B. Buell, 1904-19; Mrs. Mary B. Wilson, 1919-24; Mrs. Hattie M. Newton, 1924-26; Mrs. Lena W. Greenbacker, 1926-28; Mrs. Mary B. Wilson, 1928-29; Mrs. Mary E. Welles, 1929-35; Mrs. Ella F. Burr, 1935-45; Mrs. Norma Burgess Moore, 1945-1962; Mrs. Carrol Greene, 1962-1963; Mrs. C. Elmore Watkins, 1963-1970; Mrs. M. Allen Swift, 1970-

DELAWARE: Mrs. Sarah Bringhurst, 1880-81; Mrs. Annie H. Martindale, 1881-87; Mrs. Margaret S. Hilles, 1887-98; Mrs. E. Emma Pyle, 1898-1900; Mrs. Emma E. Caulk, 1900-09; Mrs. Kate E. Smithers, 1909-11; Mrs. Emma E. Caulk, 1911-13; Mrs. Lena Messick, 1913-19; Mrs. Georgie G. Pierce, 1919-24; Mrs. M. Evelyn Killen, 1924-29; Mrs. Anna Lee Waller, 1929 until her death, July 1944; Mrs. Katie L. B. Dockety, 1944-1951; Mrs. Helen S. Learned, 1951-1955; Mrs. Annia F. Matthews, 1955-1958; Mrs. Margaret Norris, 1958-1962; Mrs. Winfred Hilyard, 1962-1966; Mrs. Anna D. Weldin, 1966-1970; Rev. Mrs. Lorraine Ottinger, 1970-

DISTRICT OF COLUMBIA: Mrs. Julia M. Church, 1875-78; Mrs. A. M. Linville, 1878-80; Mrs. C. L. Roach, 1880-85; Mrs. S. D. LaFetra, 1885-93; Mrs. Mary E. Griffith, 1893-95; Mrs. Margaret B. Platt, 1895-98; Mrs. Clinton Smith, 1898-1911; Mrs. Emmat Sanford Shelton, 1911-25; Mrs. Nash M. Pollock, 1925-31; Mrs. Jennie Bailey Wadleigh, 1931-35; Mrs. Ida W. Ramsey, 1935-40; Mrs. Earle J. Wilfley, 1940-41; Mrs. Ida W. Ramsey, 1941-44; Mrs. Caroline E. Coates, 1944-1950; Mrs. Guy F. Grossbrenner, 1950-1956; Mrs. George A. Cook, 1956-1961; Mrs. Harry A. Rothwell, 1961-1971; Mrs. Mary McGinnis, 1971-1972; Mrs. Edward Montrose, 1972

DISTRICT OF COLUMBIA *(Frances W. Harper)*: Mrs. Sterling N. Brown, 1908-09; Mrs. Josephine B. Bruce, 1909-11; Mrs. Alma J. Scott, 1946-1948

FLORIDA: Mrs. Walter Gwynn, 1884-85; Mrs. J. L. Lyon, 1885-86; Mrs. A. A. W. Cadwallader, 1886-91; Mrs. E. A. Hill, 1891-95; Mrs. S. H. Webb, 1895-98; Mrs. Alice C. Brown, 1898-1904; Miss Minnie E. Neal, 1904-36; Mrs. Etta B. V. Mendenhall, 1936-42; Mrs. Eunice Hebb, 1942-48; Mrs. D. J. Mason, 1948-1952; Mrs. Ilean Woodruff, 1952-1954; Mrs. Florence Riggle, 1954-1962; Mrs. M. J. Maloney, 1962-

FLORIDA #2: Miss S. A. Blocker, 1902-12. Mrs. Frances E. Preston, 1919;

GEORGIA: Mrs. William C. Sibley, 1883-1900; Mrs. Jennie Hart Sibley, 1900-05; Mrs. Mary Harris Armor, 1905-09; Mrs. Thomas E. Patterson, 1909-16; Mrs. Leila A. Dillard, 1916-24; Mrs. Mary Harris Armor, 1924-26; Mrs. Marvin Williams, 1926-32; Mrs. Mary Scott Russell, 1932-1950; Mrs. H. W. Birdsong, 1950-51; Mrs. Luther Dent, 1951-1956; Mrs. W. M. Dugger, 1956-1960; Mrs. H. W. Birdsong, 1960-1964; Dr. Clare McKellar, 1965-1968; Mrs. Paris J. Watson, 1968-1972; Mrs. S. R. Clark, 1972-

GEORGIA, #2: Mrs. Georgia Swift King, 1894-95; Mrs. J. E. W. Bowen, 1897-1903; Miss Ellen Young, 1907.

HAWAII: Miss Mary E. Green, 1885-1900; Mrs. Mary S. Whitney, 1900-1920; open 1920-1925; Mrs. Allice P. Broughton, 1925-1947; Mrs. Albert S. Baker, 1947-1951; Mrs. Charles E. Hannon, 1951-1952; Mrs. Marvin Hensley, 1952-1971;

IDAHO: Mrs. J. H. Barton, 1887-88; Mrs. Henrietta Skelton, 1888-89; Mrs. Susan Holbrook, 1889-90; Mrs. Sarah Black, 1890-92; Mrs. Rebecca Mitchell, 1892-95; Mrs. J. H. Barton, 1895-97; Mrs. Neal B. Inman, 1897-1900; Mrs. Ora Oakes, 1900-01; Mrs. Sarah Mitchell, 1901-03; Mrs. Ella Crawford, 1903-04; Mrs. A. A. Garlock, 1904-08; Mrs. Nettie R. Chipp, 1908-11; Miss Daisy Beatty, 1911-12; Mrs. Nettie R. Chipp, 1912-16; Mrs. Alice Thompson, 1916-17; Dr. Emma F. A. Drake, 1917-24; Mrs. John L. Brady, 1924-34; Mrs. Josephine Roberts, 1934-36; Mrs. Margaret Palmer, 1936-39; Mrs. Bethel B. Day, 1939-43; Mrs. Mable Moody, 1943-46; Mrs. Bethel B. Day, 1946-1950; Mrs. Reed Moody, 1950-1951; Mrs. H. E. Hagedorn, 1951-1957; Mrs. Bethel B. Day, 1957-1961; Mrs. Mary V. Dunning, 1961-1963; Mrs. Mabel Roton, 1963-1966; Mrs. Mabel Robley, 1966-1972; Mrs. Ruth Heibert, 1972-

ILLINOIS: Mrs. Jennie Fowler Willing, 1874-77; Mrs. Anna M. Waite, 1877-78; Miss Frances E. Willard, 1878-79; Mrs. Elizabeth C. Hibben, 1879-82; Miss Mary Allen West, 1882-86; Mrs. Louise S. Rounds, 1886-1901; Miss Marie C. Brehm, 1901-06; Mrs. Mary E. Kuhl, 1906-11; Miss Helen L. Hood, 1911-30; Mrs. Etta Root Edwards, 1930-31; Mrs. Reed Ferguson, 1931-36; Mrs. Maude Petteys Fairbairn, 1936-46; Mrs. W. B. O'Neal, 1946-1951; Mrs. H. F. Powell, 1951-1952; Mrs. Bessie Bartlett,

1952-58; Mrs. F. B. Johnson, 1958-1960; Mrs. Robert C. Nessl, 1960-1966; Miss Juanita Whisler, 1966-

INDIANA: Mrs. Zerelda G. Wallace, 1874-76; Mrs. R. T. Brown, 1876-78; Mrs. Zerelda G. Wallace, 1878-82; Mrs. M. L. Wells, 1882-84; Mrs. J. R. Nichols, 1884-90; Mrs. Mary E. Haggart, 1890-91; Mrs. L. M. Beck, 1891-95; Mrs. Luella F. McWhirter, 1895-99; Mrs. Eunice Wilson, 1899-1902; Mrs. Culla J. Vayhinger, 1902-19; Mrs. Elizabeth T. Stanley, 1919-39; Mrs. Paul Halladay, 1939-47; Mrs. Herman Stanley, 1947-1959; Mrs. Cleo Parrish, 1959-1968; Mrs. B. B. Whitacre, 1968-

IOWA: Mrs. E. A. Wheeler, 1874-78; Mrs. V. M. Moore, 1878-82; Mrs. L. D. Carhart, 1882-84; Mrs. M. J. Aldrich, 1884-86; Mrs. J. E. Foster, 1886-91; Mrs. F. M. Hinman, 1891-98; Mrs. E. B. Hurford, 1898-1901; Mrs. Georgia Wade McClelland, 1901-04; Mrs. Florence Miller, 1904-05; Mrs. Marion H. Dunham, 1905-08; Mrs. C. B. Hurford, 1908-13; Mrs. Ida B. Wise Smith, 1913-33; Mrs. Jeannette H. Mann, 1933-36; Mrs. Harry G. McCullough, 1936-43; Mrs. Lydia Stotts, 1943-44; Mrs. Ida B. Wise Smith, 1944-45; Mrs. Gertrude H. Walton, 1945-1952; Mrs. Bertha Klousia, 1952-1960; Mrs. Lelah Rich, 1960-61; Rev. Mrs. Emma A. Arnold, 1961-1966; Mrs. Cecil Roberts, 1966-1971; Mrs. Marion Schippers, 1971-

KANSAS: Mrs. M. B. Smith, 1879; Mrs. Druscilla Wilson, 1879-82; Mrs. H. C. Fields, 1882-84; Mrs. Fannie Rastall, 1884-91; Mrs. F. S. Grubb, 1891-93; Mrs. L. B. Smith, 1893-96; Mrs. Ella W. Brown, 1896-99; Mrs. E. P. Hutchinson, 1899-1909; Mrs. Lillian M. Mitchner, 1909-38; Mrs. Agnes D. Hays, 1938-44; Mrs. Edna F. Davidson, 1944-46; Mrs. Mable M. Gilbert, 1946-1951; Mrs. Anna R. Lambert, 1951-1960; Mrs. Winifred B. Petterson, 1960-1970; Mrs. James Hatfield, 1970-

KENTUCKY: Mrs. Julia Shaw, half of year 1881; Mrs. George A. Bain, 1881-88; Mrs. Lucy B. Neal, part of year 1888; Mrs. Mamie Nonnell, 1888-90; Frances E. Beauchamp, 1890-1923; Mrs. Lucy Lee Mahan Spillman, 1923-24; Mrs. Ludie Day Pickett, 1924-47; Mrs. E. D. Hinkle, 1947-1966; Mrs. Hugh Clark, 1966-1970; Mrs. Mitylene Holmes, 1970-

KENTUCKY *(Sojourner Truth)*: Mrs. L. B. Fouse, 1945-1953; Mrs. Decora Williams, 1953-1957;

LOUISIANA: Mrs. Caroline M. Merrick, 1883-89; Mrs. Mary D. Goodale, 1889-99; Miss Mae Walker, 1899-1900; Mrs. Alice Zable, 1900-

02; Mrs. E. F. Blanks, 1902-05; Mrs. Nellie O'Beirne, 1905-07; Mrs. Kate Wilkins, 1907-09; Mrs. Alice McKinney, 1909-28; Mrs. Lula Collins, 1928-34; Mrs. Maude Eglin, 1934-36; Mrs. Beulah Mayo, 1936-42; Mrs. Texye Riddle, 1942-43; Mrs. Morris Hudson, 1943-44; Mrs. J. W. Worthington, 1944-48; Mrs. C. A. Phillips, 1948-1950; Mrs. Fred St. Amant, 1950-1953; Mrs. Harvey Hall, 1952-1956; Mrs. L. B. Miller, 1956-1963; Mrs. H. M. Tripp, 1963-1966; Mrs. E. W. Dossett, 1966-1969; Mrs. Lloyd Pye, 1969-1970; Mrs. E. W. Dossett, 1970-

LOUISIANA *(Frances Willard)*: Mrs. Frances Joseph, 1898-1904; Mrs. Frances J. Gaudet, 1904-19.

MAINE: Mrs. Charles F. Allen, 1875-78; Mrs. Lillian M. N. Stevens, 1878-1914; Mrs. Althea G. Quimby, 1914-39; Mrs. Augusta K. Christie, 1939-1960; Mrs. Benjamin J. Sweet, 1960-1967; Mrs. Edward McGuiggan, 1967—

MARYLAND: Mrs. Francis T. Crook, 1875-78; Mrs. Mary Whitall Thomas, 1878-88; Mrs. Juliet Sewell Baldwin, 1888-94; Mrs. Mary Rider Haslup, 1894-1936; Miss Bertha M. Tyson, 1936-46; Mrs. Charles H. Wagner, 1946-1954; Miss Ada B. Wooden, 1954-1958; Mrs. Melvin E. Lederer, 1958-1969; Mrs. Lewis Shannahan, 1969-

Maryland, #2: Mrs. Margaret Peck Hill, 1915-44; Mrs. Annie E. S. Wells, 1944-1964;

MASSACHUSETTS: Mrs. Susan A. Gifford, 1874-75; Mrs. Mary A. Livermore, 1875-84; Miss Elizabeth S. Tobey, 1884-90; Mrs. Susan S. Fessenden, 1890-98; Mrs. Katharine Lente Stevenson, 1898-1918; Mrs. Ella A. Gleason, 1918-22; Mrs. Alice G. Ropes, 1922-38; Mrs. Lila D. Warren, 1938-47; Mrs. Minnie E. Graves, 1947-1954; Mrs. Julia B. Kohler, 1954-1963; Mrs. R. Margaret Webber, 1963-1969; Mrs. Lawrence I. Moore, 1969-

MICHIGAN: Mrs. H. A. Tracy, 1874-75; Mrs. A. F. Bourns, 1875-76; Mrs. B. B. Hudson, 1876-81; Mrs. Mary T. Lathrap, 1881-95; Mrs. A. J. Benjamin, 1895-1905; Mrs. Emor L. Calkins, 1905-26; Mrs. Elizabeth Perkins, 1926-27; Mrs. Stella Roben, 1927-31; Mrs. Dora B. Whitney, 1931-47; Mrs. O. R. Hurd, 1947-1957; Mrs. L. G. Rowley, 1957-1964; Mrs. Parker Tagsold, 1964-1966; Mrs. Chester Walker, 1966-

MINNESOTA: Mrs. W. Holt, 1877-78; Mrs. A. T. Anderson, 1878-79; Mrs. S. H. Barteau, 1879-80; Mrs. A. T. Anderson, 1880-81; Mrs. Harriet

A. Hobart, 1881-94; Mrs. Susanna M. D. Fry, 1894-97; Mrs. Bessie Lathe Scovell, 1897-1909; Miss Rozette Hendrix, 1909-21; Mrs. Josephine E. Sizer, 1921-31; Mrs. Harriet G. Northfield, 1931-35; Mrs. Ethel Bliss Baker, 1935-46; Mrs. Maude E. Teigan, 1946-1950; Mrs. Erma Van De Walker, 1950-1952; Ethel Bliss Baker, 1952-1954; Mrs. Ruth Tollefson, 1954-1955; Mrs. Maude E. Teigan, 1955-1959; Mrs. J. H. Grostephan, 1959-1960; Mrs. Esther Tideman, 1960 1964; Mrs. Wallace Johnson, 1964-1967; Mrs. Wilbur T. Geary, 1967-

MISSISSIPPI: Mrs. A. P. Stewart, 1883-84; Mrs. Ellen Frances Steel, 1884-85; Mrs. F. H. Ervin, 1885-87; Mrs. M. E. Ervin, 1887-89; Mrs. L. S. Mount, 1889-96; Mrs. Mary B. Curlee, 1896-99; Mrs. M. L. Montgomery, 1899-1900; Mrs. Mary B. Curlee, 1900-01; Mrs. Harriet B. Kells, 1901-06; Mrs. Fannie S. Clark, 1906-07; Mrs. Harriet B. Kells, 1907-15; Mrs. S. E. Stanley, 1915-18; Miss Madge Montgomery, 1918-19; Miss Helen P. Woodward, 1919-23; Mrs. Clara P. Cox, 1923-24; Mrs. W. E. Sigler, 1924-25; Mrs. Nellie N. Sommerville, 1925-30; Mrs. W. Q. Sharp, 1930-34; Mrs. R. L. Ezelle, 1934-39; Miss Susie Powell, 1939-46; Mrs. Adele C. Baker, 1946-1949; Mrs. R. L. Ezelle, 1949-1957; Mrs. J. A. Burt, 1957-1958; Mrs. J. E. Crymes, 1958-1966; Mrs. George Vinzant, 1966-1969; Mrs. Robert E. Rodgers, 1969-

MISSISSIPPI, #2: Mrs. Desney Jones, 1900-01; Mrs. S. E. Desney, 1901-03; Mrs. Ardelle E. Walker, 1950-1951.

MISSOURI: Mrs. Mary M. Clardy, April to October, 1882; Mrs. Clara C. Hoffman, 1882-1901; Mrs. Belle C. Kimball, 1901-03; Mrs. Clara C. Hoffman, 1903-08; Mrs. Carrie Lee Carter Stokes, 1908-09; Mrs. Kate F. Newton, 1909-13; Mrs. Nelle G. Burger, 1913-47; Mrs. B. Blanche Butts, 1947-1950; Mrs. Robert C. Young, 1950-1952; Mrs. B. B. Butts-Runion, 1952-1956; Mrs. J. E. Plummer, 1956-1960; Mrs. LAN Nielsen, 1960-1966; Mrs. Galen Huffman, 1966-1972; Mrs. W. E. Chandler, 1972-

MISSOURI (*Sojourner Truth*): Mrs. M. R. Jordan, 1947-48; Mrs. Ralph Davy, 1948-1951; Mrs. Ardelle Walker, 1951-1954; Mrs. Mary T. Dreer, 1954-1958.

MONTANA: Mrs. R. F. Clark, 1883-84; Mrs. G. B. Morse, 1884-85; Mrs. Laura E. Howey, 1885-90; Mrs. M. S. Cummins, 1890-94; Mrs. Mary A. Wylie, 1894-96; Rev. Alice S. N. Barnes, 1896-1900; Mrs. Anna A. Walker, 1900-02; Mrs. I. N. Smith, 1902-04; Mrs. W. E. Currah, 1904-08;

Rev. Alice Barnes Hoag, 1908-09; Mrs. Allie U. Hutchinson, 1909-13; Mrs. Mary L. Alderson, 1913-17; Mrs. Anna G. Herbst, 1917-19; Mrs. Mary Stranahan, 1919-21; Mrs. J. E. Cocks, 1921-24; Mrs. W. C. Dawes, 1924-37; Mrs. H. E. Chappell, 1937-1940; Mrs. E. Pease, 1940-46; Mrs. H. C. Kreis, 1946-1952; Mrs. E. B. Noble, 1952-1956; Mrs. H. B. Henricksen, 1956-1960; Mrs. Richard E. Clarke, 1960-1963; Mrs. E. H. Rigby, 1963-1966; Mrs. Harry Henderson, 1966-1968; Mrs. O. A. Perkins, 1968-

NEBRASKA: Mrs. Anton Brown, 1875-76; Mrs. Charlotte Hardy, 1876-81; Mrs. Jennie Ford, 1881-84; Mrs. Jennie Holmes, 1884-88; Mrs. Mary Hitchcock, 1888-94; Mrs. Susannah Walker, 1894-1902; Mrs. Dora V. Wheelock, 1902-06; Mrs. Frances B. Heald, 1906-13; Mrs. Mamie Claflin, 1913-19; Mrs. Lela G. Dyar, 1919-25; Mrs. Clara S. Clayton, 1925-31; Rev. Iva M. Innis, 1931-37; Mrs. Mary L. Seibert, 1937-43; Mrs. Katherine M. Rose, 1943-44; Mrs. Mabel M. Nylander, 1944-47; Mrs. Myrtle E. Davidson, 1947-1950; Mrs. Roy A. Jones, 1950-51; Mrs. Nettie Ring, 1951-1955; Mrs. Myrtle E. Davidson, 1955-1959; Mrs. R. Lee Gilmer, 1959-1964; Mrs. Ella Melton-Peck, 1964-1969; Mrs. Fred Patzell, 1969-

NEVADA: Mrs. H. Elizabeth Webster, 1883-86; Mrs. Lucy Van De-Venter, 1886-91; Mrs. Clara S. Ward, 1891-93; Mrs. Lucy Van DeVenter, 1893-94; Dr. Eliza Cook, 1894-97; Mrs. Florence A. Church, 1897-1901; Mrs. Nettie P. Hershiser, 1901-12; Mrs. Nora R. Linville, 1912-19; Mrs. Maude C. Edwards, 1919-22; Mrs. Winnie R. Steinbeck, 1922-24; Mrs. Maude C. Edwards, 1924-25; Mrs. Alexinia McNabey (acting pres.), 1925-26; Mrs. R. L. Macy, 1926-27; Mrs. Clara Angell (acting pres.), 1927-28; Mrs. Ada Williams, 1928-29; Mrs. George W. Lattin, 1929-32; Mrs. Thurlow Douglas, 1932-33; Mrs. Mary Franzman, 1933-35; Mrs. Thurlow Douglas, 1935-36; Mrs. T. V. Connor, 1936-39; Mrs. Howard K. Arentz, 1939-42; Mrs. Susan Russell, 1942-43; Mrs. Zua J. Harding, 1943-44; Mrs. Elva E. Duncan, 1944-45; Mrs. Bessie Menke, 1945-47; Mrs. Sophia E. Riggle, 1947-1948; Mrs. Bessie Menke, 1948-1949; Mrs. Harriet Arentz, 1949-1961; Mrs. Ethel Conley, 1961-1962; Mrs. Florence Marsh, 1962-1966; Mrs. Edith Gamos, 1966-1967; Mrs. Samuel Arentz, 1967-

NEW HAMPSHIRE: Mrs. A. S. White, 1874-78; Miss Abbie McIntire, 1878-81; Mrs. Janette Hill Knox, 1881-92; Miss C. R. Wendell, 1892-99; Mrs. Ellen R. Richardson, 1899-1920; Mrs. Charline M. Abbott, 1920-31; Mrs. Gertrude W. Osborne, 1931-39; Mrs. Grace M. Hamilton, 1939-46;

Mrs. Minnie L. Caswell, 1946-1952; Mrs. Faye N. Child, 1952-1957; Mrs. Marian G. Campbell, 1957-

NEW JERSEY: Mrs. Mary R. Denman, 1874-80; Mrs. S. J. C. Downs, 1880-91; Mrs. Emma Bourne, 1891-1910; Miss Esther H. Elfreth, 1910 (half year) 1924; Mrs. Eva E. Gebhardt (half year) 1924; Mrs. Nina G. Frantz, 1924-35; Mrs. Ada S. Nodocker, 1935-39; Mrs. Mary D. DuBois, 1939-48; Mrs. Ella P. Christner, 1948-1956; Mrs. Elwood Du Bois, 1956-1959; Mrs. Elgin R. Mayer, 1959-1967; Mrs. Samuel A. Jeanes, 1967-

NEW MEXICO: Miss Mary L. Brown, 1882-83; Mrs. Gen. Sheldon, 1883-84; Mrs. Evelyn Snyder, 1884-85; Mrs. P. E. Collings, 1885-89; Mrs. M. C. Raynolds, 1889-90; Mrs. M. J. Borden, 1890-1902; Mrs. B. Emma Marshall, 1902-03; Rev. Mary J. Borden, 1903-06; Mrs. S. C. Nutter, 1906-12; Mrs. A. A. Scott, 1912-14; Miss Harriet L. Henderson, 1914-17; Mrs. S. C. Nutter, 1917-19; Mrs. Anna W. Strumquist, 1919-22; Mrs. Lilie C. Harrison, 1922-24; Mrs. Anna W. Strumquist, 1924-25; Mrs. Dehlia Wingo, 1925-33; Dr. Eleanor James, 1933-34; Mrs. W. C. Holland, 1934-41; Mrs. George A. Endicott, 1941-42; Mrs. Dan W. Palmer, 1942-46; Mrs. Viola Sides, 1946-47; Mrs. M. M. Ward, 1947-1950; Mrs. H. T. Williams, 1950-1952; Mrs. E. J. Galloway, 1952-1956; Mrs. Esther Burch, 1956-1959; Mrs. Opal Heath, 1959-1963; Mrs. F. E. Wilson, 1963-1967; Mrs. James Jenkins, 1967-1968; Mrs. E. F. Galloway, 1968-1971; Mrs. Alfred Collins, 1971-

NEW YORK: Mrs. Allen Butler, 1874-79; Mrs. F. G. Hibbard, 1879-82; Mrs. Mary T. Burt, 1882-97; Mrs. Ella A. Boole, 1897-1903; Mrs. Frances W. Graham, 1903-09; Mrs. Ella A. Boole, 1909-26; Mrs. D. Leigh Colvin, 1926-44; Miss Helen G. H. Estelle, 1944-1956; Mrs. Hazel C. Wells, 1956-1960; Mrs. Rachel Waters, 1960-

NORTH CAROLINA: Mrs. A. L. Wright, 1883-84; Mrs. Mary Woody, 1884-94; Mrs. Mary Cartland, 1894-1902; Mrs. C. E. Craven, 1902-04; Miss Elizabeth March, 1904-05; Mrs. Laura Winston, 1905-06; Miss Elizabeth March, 1906-08; Miss Elizabeth Moore, 1908-10; Miss Eula Dixon, 1910-11; Mrs. T. Adelaide Goodno, 1911-24; Mrs. W. B. Lindsay, 1924-37; Mrs. T. H. Plemmons, 1937-41; Mrs. L. E. Brown, 1941-1950; Mrs. W. H. Causey, 1950-1952; Mrs. L. V. Scott, 1952-1960; Mrs. J. B. Davis, 1960-

NORTH CAROLINA #2: Mrs. M. J. O'Connell, 1890-94; Mrs. Mary A. Lynch, 1897-1917; (*Sojourner Truth*) Mrs. Janie S. Thomas, 1947-1970.

NORTH DAKOTA: Miss Adelaide M. Kinnear, 1889-93; Mrs. Elizabeth Preston Anderson, 1893-1933; Mrs. Fred M. Wanner, 1933-39; Mrs. Bessie M. Darling, 1939-47; Mrs. H. E. Mielke, 1947-1952; Mrs. A. D. Ottinger, 1952-1969; Rev. Eva M. Peet, 1969-1971; Mrs. L. Roy Bartle, 1971-

OHIO: Mrs. Harriet C. McCabe, 1874-79; Mrs. Mary A. Woodbridge, 1879-86; Mrs. Henrietta L. Monroe, 1886-97; Mrs. Anna W. Clark, 1897-07; Mrs. Frances Ensign Fuller, 1907-12; Mrs. Florence D. Richard, 1912-32; Mrs. Viola D. Romans, 1932-39; Miss Mary B. Ervin, 1939-1952; Mrs. Esther M. Madsen, 1952-1959; Mrs. Harold H. Brown, 1959-1967; Mrs. Albert Shoemaker, 1967-1972; Mrs. Paul Lafferty, 1972-

OKLAHOMA: started as Indian Territory, Mrs. Jane Stapler (Cherokee Indian princess), 1888-98; Mrs. Eva Ratcliff, 1898-1900; Mrs. K. L. E. Murrow, 1900-01;Mrs. Laura Harsha, 1901-06; Mrs. Lilah D. Lindsay, 1906-07; united with Oklahoma, which started with Mrs. W. L. Rhodes, 1889-90; Mrs. A. G. Murray, 1890-91; Mrs. J. E. Roberts, 1891-92; Mrs. Nellie Sheplor, 1892-93; Mrs. Matilda Switzer, 1893-94; Mrs. Amelia Mentz, 1894-96; Mrs. Sue Uhl Brown, 1896-97; Mrs. Susie B. Jackson. 1897-98; Mrs. Katherine Ferguson, 1898-99; Mrs. Dorothy J. Cleveland, 1899-1903; Mrs. Abbie Hillerman, 1903-07; Mrs. Cora D. Hammett, 1907-10; Mrs. Abbie Hillerman, 1910-19; Mrs. Josephine M. Buhl, 1919-28; Mrs. Elizabeth House, 1928-1962; Mrs. Dee Whitby, 1962-64; Mrs. E. H. Smith. 1964-1971; Mrs. Ellen Murphy, 1971-

OKLAHOMA *(Sojourner Truth)*: Mrs. M. L. Sanders, 1947-1962; Mrs. M. E. Burrow, 1962-1966.

OREGON: Mrs. E. J. G. Hines, 1883-85; Mrs. Anna R. Riggs, 1885-93; Mrs. Narcissa W. Kinney, 1893-99; Mrs. Helen D. Harford, 1899-1903; Mrs. L. H. Additon, 1903-06; Mrs. Henrietta Brown, 1906-08; Mrs. Ada Wallace Unruh, 1908-12; Rev. Edith Hill-Booker, 1912-13; Mrs. Jennie M. Kemp, 1913-16; Mrs. M. Frances Swope, 1916-17; Mrs. Mattie Sleeth, 1917-19; Mrs. Mary L. Mallett, 1919-27; Mrs. Ada Jolley, 1927-35; Mrs. Rachel Ellis, 1935-36; Mrs. Necia E. Buck, 1936-41; Mrs. Fred J. Tooze, 1941-1957; Mrs. William Hargis, 1959-1963; Mrs. Eldon Helm, 1963-

PENNSYLVANIA: Mrs. Fannie B. Chase, 1874-79; Mrs. A. C. Law, 1879-80; Mrs. Francis L. Swift, 1880-89; Mrs. Mary H. Jones, 1889-92; Mrs. Anna M. Hammer, 1892-97; Mrs. Rebecca B. Chambers, 1897-1907;

Mrs. Ella M. George, 1907-1929; Mrs. Ella B. Black, 1929-1949; Mrs. A. F. Leonhard, 1949-1957; Mrs. Martha B. Mayhugh, 1957-1962; Mrs. Lois Mason, 1962-1968; Mrs. Samuel T. Dundore, 1968-

PUERTO RICO: Mrs. Edith Wardell Hildreth, 1915-21; Mrs. Edith M. Irvine-Rivera, 1921-30; Miss Rena Thistleton, 1930-35; Mrs. Edith M. Irvine-Rivera, 1935-1953; Mrs. Berta O. de Castro, 1953-1957; Mrs. Angela Diaz de Gutrierrez, 1957-1958; Mrs. Elizabeth Mendez de Pales, 1958-1963; Mrs. Santia Pagan, 1963-1966; Mrs. Ramonita Rivera, 1969-1970; Mrs. Clara Farrar de Cancel, 1970-1972; Mrs. Ramonita Rivera, 1972-

RHODE ISLAND: Mrs. Lucy Bainbridge, part of 1875; Miss Phebe Hathaway, 1875-77; Mrs. J. K. Barney, 1877-84; Mrs. Emeline Burlingame, 1884-90; Mrs. Mary Babcock, 1890-1904; Mrs. Deborah K. Livingston, 1904-13; Mrs. Jennie L. W. Rooke, 1913-19; Mrs. Ethelyn Roberts, 1919-30; Mrs. Grace Barber, 1930-31; Mrs. Grace Drown, 1931-36; Mrs. Mary M. Eldridge, 1936-44; Mrs. Jennie H. Nichols, 1944-1952; Mrs. Margaret Collings, 1953-1959; Miss Frances E. Smith, 1959-1960; Mrs. Barbara Snyder, 1960-1963; Mrs. Inez Wilson, 1963-1966; Mrs. Alice T. Harnett, 1966-1967; Mrs. Florence Suetterlien, 1967-1972; Mrs. Edith Naylor, 1972-

SOUTH CAROLINA: Mrs. Sallie F. Chapin, 1882-96; Mrs. Lucius Roach, 1896-99; Mrs. Betty Pace Hayes, 1899-1901; Mrs. Janie Herbert Haynes, 1901-06; Mrs. Joseph Sprott, 1906-28; Mrs. J. L. Mims, 1928-45; Mrs. Harry Gandy, 1945-47; Mrs. A. D. Betts, 1947—

SOUTH CAROLINA *(Lawson)*: Mrs. E. V. C. Williams, 1907-14; Mrs. L. A. J. Moorer, 1916-30.

SOUTH DAKOTA: Mrs. Helen M. Barker, 1886-92; Mrs. Emma A. Crammer, 1892-95; Mrs. Luella A. Ramsey, 1895-1905; Mrs. Anna R. Simmons, 1909-17; Mrs. Flora A. Mitchell, 1917-41; Mrs. Mary S. Lyman, 1941-47; Mrs. Ruth Martin, 1947-48; Mrs. Robert Fortner, 1948-1960; Mrs. Arthur Winquist, 1960-1967; Mrs. Emil Bechtle, 1967-1972; Mrs. Loyd Lettelier, 1972-

TENNESSEE: Mrs. J. C. Johnson, 1882-83; Mrs. Ellen Harrison, 1883-84; Mrs. Lide Merriwether, 1884-96; Mrs. A. A. Gibson, 1896-98; Mrs. S. M. Holman, 1898-1914; Mrs. Mary P. Bang, 1914-16; Mrs. Minnie Alison Welch, 1916-45; Mrs. C. V. Biddle, 1945-1954; Mrs. S. C. Beard, 1954-1971; Mrs. Wayne Blankenship, 1971-

TENNESSEE, #2: Mrs. Lucy E. T. Phillips, 1897-1901; Mrs. Virginia

Broughton, 1901-11; Mrs. N. E. Davis, 1911-13; Mrs. J. W. Sexton, 1913-1915; Mrs. I. L. Inman, 1915-17; *(Sojourner Truth)* Mrs. Bertha C. Singleton, 1945-1953; Mrs. J. H. Colman, 1953-1967;

TEXAS: Mrs. Jennie Bland Beauchamp, 1883-88; Mrs. S. C. Acheson, 1888-91; Mrs. Helen M. Stoddard, 1891-07; Mrs. Mattie R. Turner, 1907-08; Mrs. J. B. Ammerman, 1908-09; Mrs. Nannie W. Curtis, 1909-20; Mrs. Cora McGrail, 1920-22; Mrs. Claude De Van Watts, 1922-1961; Mrs. Ruth Horner Godbey, 1961-

TEXAS *(Thurman)*: Mrs. E. E. Peterson, 1899-1914; Mrs. M. J. Turner, 1914-15; Mrs. M. J. Turner Campbell, 1915-16; *(Sojourner Truth)*, Mrs. Carrie E. Martin, 1945-1965.

UTAH: Mrs. Major Dewey, 1877-78; Mrs. Elmira Losee, 1878-80; Mrs. M. E. B. Greene, 1880-81; Mrs. J. C. Royle, 1881-83; Miss Lydia E. Payne, 1883-86; Miss E. S. Dickey, 1886-87; Mrs. A. A. Hawkes, 1887-88, Mrs. L. M. Bailey, 1888-92; Mrs. Caroline H. Reed, 1892-93; Mrs. Hester T. Griffith, 1893-94; Mrs. G. W. Martin, 1894-98; Mrs. Frances C. Smith, 1898-1902; Mrs. J. S. Gordon, 1902-05; Mrs. Lulu L. Shepard, 1905-16; Mrs. C. A. Walker, 1916-21; Mrs. D. W. Jenkins, 1921-25; Mrs. M. H. Parry, 1925-30; Mrs. D. W. Jenkins, 1930-41; Mrs. Alice M. Ault, 1941-46; Rev. May Frazee, 1946-48; Mrs. John Latimer, Jr., 1948-1955; Mrs. Lois L. Hubbard, 1955-1957; Lucinda Jensen, 1957-1960; Mrs. R. E. Nelson, 1960-1963;

VERMONT: Mrs. E. B. Taplin, 1874-75; Mrs. M. F. Perkins, 1875-76; Mrs. J. M. Haven, 1876-78; Mrs. M. F. Perkins, 1878-79; Mrs. Anna C. Park, 1879-81; Mrs. E. C. Greene, 1881-85; Mrs. J. L. Perkins, 1885-87; Mrs. E. T. Housh, 1887-92; Mrs. Ida H. Read, 1892-1908; Mrs. Gratia Davidson, 1908-13; Mrs. Minnie L. Pearson, 1913-20; Mrs. Elsie Pease Barney, 1920-29; Mrs. Ida M. Cutler, 1929-32; Mrs. Ellen W. Miller, 1932-38; Mrs. Nettie B. Shedd-Kidder, 1938-1949; Mrs. Goldie Welch, 1949-1956; Miss Lettie Foster, 1956-1960; Mrs. Everett Chase, 1960-

VIRGINIA: Mrs. William H. Pleasants, January to October 1883; Mrs. Rebecca D. Wilson, October 1883-86; Mrs. William H. Pleasants, 1886-88; Mrs. R. H. Jones, 1888-98; Mrs. Howard M. Hoge, 1898-1938; Mrs. Amy C. Weech, 1938-42; Mrs. Herbert W. Phillips, 1942-1951; Mrs. T. Roy Jarrett, 1951-1959; Mrs. R. G. Farrar, 1959-1963; Mrs. Carlisle Williams, 1963-1966; Mrs. O. R. Clark, 1966-1970; Mrs. J. Buhl, Sr., 1970-

VIRGINIA, #2: Mrs. Rosa D. Bowser, 1902-11; Mrs. Lucy B. Stephens, 1911-13; *(Sojourner Truth)* Mrs. C. E. Jones, 1946-1953; Mrs. Daisy Schley, 1953-1958; Mrs. Emily O. L. Price, 1958-1968.

WASHINGTON (East): Mrs. T. R. Tannat, 1883-84; Mrs. Eliza Cobleigh, March to July 1884; Mrs. Lucy A. R. Switzer, 1884-92; Mrs. Anna C. Singer, part of year, 1892; Mrs. Amanda Strong, 1892-93; Mrs. Jennie L. Green, 1893-94; Mrs. Julia Cole, 1894-95; Mrs. Delia C. H. Cox, 1895-99; Mrs. Fannie M. Clark, 1899-1900; Mrs. E. C. Bodwell, 1900-09; Mrs. Anna Angier, 1909-12; Mrs. Carrie M. Barr, 1912-21; Mrs. Allie Methven, 1921-23; Miss Edith Whiting, 1923-28; Mrs. Martha P. Murray, April to October 1928; Mrs. Ida S. Gage, 1928-31; Mrs. Martha P. Murray, 1931-41; Mrs. Ruby Railsback, 1941-1955; Mrs. T. C. Wurth, 1955-1966; Mrs. Lendabell Schmid, 1966-

WASHINGTON (West): Mrs. Margaret LeSourd, part of 1883; Mrs. Winnie Thomas, 1883-86; Mrs. Carrie M. White, 1886-87; Mrs. M. A. Shaffer, 1887-95; Miss Mary L. Page, 1895-1900; Mrs. Margaret B. Platt, 1900-15; Mrs. Harriet B. Dunlap, 1915-17; Miss Mary E. Brown, 1917-22; Mrs. Lillian M. Vincent, 1922-36; Mrs. Ella H. Booker, 1936-39; Mrs. Winifred M. Lewis, 1939-47; Mrs. Maude M. Isaacs, 1947-1953; Mrs. Charles Budde, 1953-

WEST VIRGINIA: Miss Amanda Taylor, 1883-85; Mrs. Jane A. Johnson, 1885-90; Mrs. Jennie P. Sisson, 1890-94; Mrs. N. R. C. Morrow, 1894-1904; Mrs. Francis P. Parks, 1904-08; Mrs. Lenna Lowe Yost, 1908-19; Mrs. Olive C. Barnes, 1919-29; Mrs. Blanche M. Pickering, 1929-32; Mrs. Ernest Henson, 1932-43; Mrs. F. L. Miller, 1943-48; Mrs. A. L. Rohrer, 1948-1959; Mrs. W. H. Robinson, 1959-1963; Mrs. C. B. Mason, 1963-1968; Mrs. Kelly Williams, 1968-

WEST VIRGINIA, #2: Miss Mary E. K. Brady, 1911-12.

WISCONSIN: Mrs. Susan B. Steele, 1874-78; Mrs. W. H. Hinckley, 1878-80; Mrs. W. A. Marshall, 1880-82; Mrs. Isabelle H. Irish, 1882-84; Miss Amy Kellogg, 1884-88; Mrs. Amy Kellogg Morse, 1888-92; Mrs. Vie Campbell, 1892-98; Mrs. Mary C. Upham, 1898-1907; Mrs. W. A. Lawson, 1907-18; Mrs. Mary Scott Johnson, 1918-24; Mrs. Annie W. Warren, 1924-32; Mrs. Mildred E. Hopkins, 1932-41; Mrs. Emma Mielkie, 1941-1950; Mrs. Olive Fisher, 1950-1958; Mrs. Bertha Meinert, 1958-1966; Mrs. Pearl Flugum, 1966-1970; Rev. Miss Norma Henderson, 1970-

WYOMING: Mrs. Judge Browne, 1883-84; Mrs. E. S. Boyd, 1884-87; Mrs. William Hicks, 1887-88; Miss L. Annette Northrup, 1888-89; Mrs. O. L. Fisher, 1889-91; Miss L. Annette Northrup, 1891-92; Mrs. Wilhelmina Brown, 1892-95; Mrs. C. M. Lusk, 1895-96; Mrs. F. A. Jones, 1896-98; Mrs. Caria Simpson, 1898-99; Mrs. Nina Higby, 1899-1904; Mrs. Alice C. Hays, 1904 05; Mrs. Dollie Legate, 1905-06; Ellen J. Wetlaufer, M.D., 1906-15; Mrs. Anna Allison, 1915-18; Mrs. Vesta Tyson, 1918-19; Mrs. Sarah E. Bailey, 1919-23; Mrs. Minnie Fenwick, 1923-30; Mrs. Pearl Ferguson, 1930-35; Mrs. Meroa E. Thomas, 1935-38; Mrs. Sarah E. Bailey, 1938-39; Mrs. Nellie Lewis, 1939-40; Mrs. Sarah E. Bailey, 1940-41; Mrs. Nellie E. Lewis, 1941-47; Mrs. Murriel J. Woods, 1947-1963; Mrs. J. E. Overstreet, 1963-

INDEX

Technical Advisor; Michael Carlucci Vitucci,
Managing Editor of The Union Signal and Young Crusader